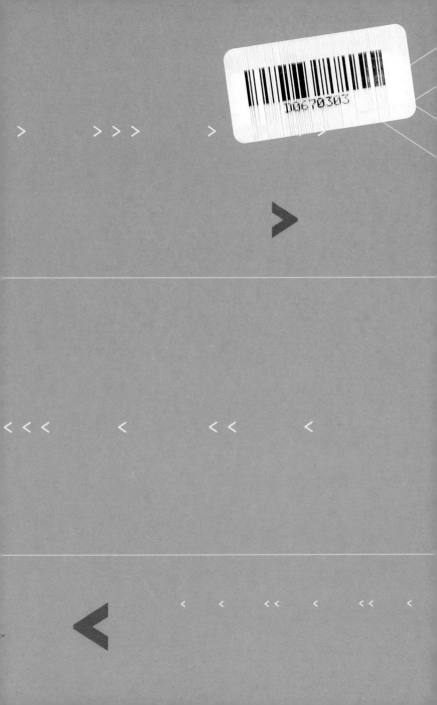

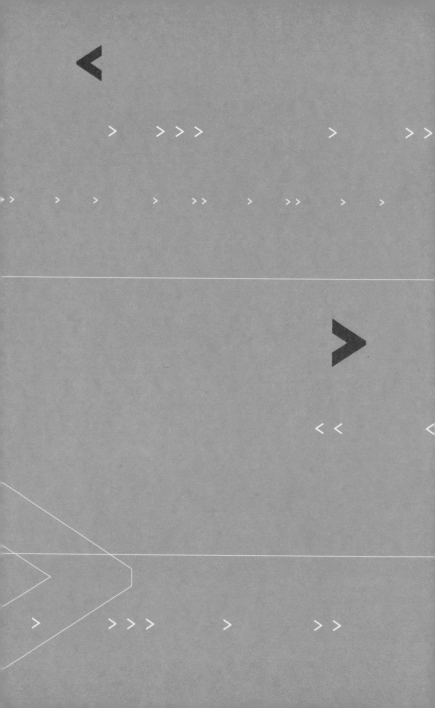

endorsements

> >   >   >   > >   > >

"Jill Ewert is arguably the world's leading Christian sports journalist, and over the past nine years, has interviewed many of God's best athletes in the spotlight. Now, in *Sharing the Victory: Being Your Best for God*, Jill takes us into the spiritual struggles and victories of the greatest Christian athletes serving Christ today through sports. If you want to escape mediocrity in your athletics or in life, a journey through *Sharing the Victory* is a great first step. I recommend taking the journey with a friend or two so you can encourage each other along the way."

—*Ron Forseth, Vice President, Outreach, Inc.*

"Jill Ewert is a godly, enthusiastic lover of Jesus. The overflow of who she is in Christ is reflected in her great love for seeing those in the sports world follow Christ. Jill's snapshot of some of our greatest athletes' and coaches' pursuit of Jesus is inspiring. But what I love about these devotions most is that the arrow points right back to me with each one, challenging and inspiring me to follow Jesus with everything I've got."

—*Ron Brown, Running Backs Coach, University of Nebraska*

"Throughout my career in Major League Baseball, I have both seen and experienced the enormous pressure to perform that is put on athletes and coaches. It's important that they have a firm foundation in something other than the stat sheet in order to stay mentally and spiritually healthy. Through *Sharing the Victory: Being Your Best for God*, athletes and coaches will be encouraged by the truth that their true value and worth come not from the scoreboard, but from the God who loves them."

—*Dayton Moore, General Manager, Kansas City Royals*

"As the CEO of the National Center for Fathering, I am always encouraged to see resources that will help men and women be the godly role models they were created to be. I truly believe that *Sharing the Victory: Being Your Best for God* by my dear friend Jill Ewert fits that description in a powerful way by providing faith lessons from influential athletes and coaches. Because today's society puts such emphasis on athletics, I believe this is an important and relevant tool for reaching not only fathers, but anyone who speaks the universal language of sports."

—*Carey Casey, CEO, National Center for Fathering*

"In our society, we get pushed to be the best, to be number 1, when we really should strive to be the best *we* can be. Jill gets it. She challenges us to be the best for God alone, not others. What a powerful reminder that we play and live for Him. If you want to grow, dig into this book! It will make a difference!"

—*Dan Britton, Executive Vice President,*
Fellowship of Christian Athletes

> >   >   >   > >   >   >

Sharing the Victory: Being Your Best for God is much more than a devotional. It is both an opportunity to draw near to God and be completely transformed by Him, and also a personal look into the hearts of professional athletes who love and live for Jesus. Through these faith lessons, I pray that God will open up the doors into your own life and create an environment where He can come in and challenge you, encourage you, and mold you into the best possible YOU. It will hands-down leave you expecting 100 percent of God's goodness for your life and, hopefully, a fresh desire to live fully and boldly for Him. May God bless you through this journey."

—Kate Ridnour, wife of NBA guard Luke Ridnour,
and former college volleyball player

"Jill Ewert has been given a special gift by God to draw her readers closer to Him. Through Jill's role as editor of *Sharing the Victory* magazine and now her new devotional book, she brings the stories of faith and sports together in order to inspire her readers to live more for the Master. You will be blessed by reading and studying this great, new book!"

—David Daly, National Director, FCA Baseball

"Jill Ewert offers a fresh and interesting way for daily reflection. The lives of faithful athletes become an encouragement for anyone who finds themselves in the tension between Christ and competition. Paul said of the faithful of his day, 'Hold men like him in high regard' (Philippians 2:29). We see God's holiness in His Son and also through the lives of the faithful, in both Scripture and those of our day. Each devotional will give a fresh insight into the Christian lives of athletes who have 'run with endurance.'"

—*Tommy Nelson, Senior Pastor, Denton Bible Church*

"Jill catches both the professional and spiritual essence of the athletes she features in this book. They become more personal and personable as she links their athletic abilities, achievements, and challenges with their faith-walk. Jill develops each feature into a scripturally-based, meaty devotion suited for men and women alike, athlete or not. Well done, Jill!"

—*Judy Rossi, author and Founder of Enhancing Your Marriage and Family Ministries*

"Hebrews 10:24 tells us to 'consider how we may spur one another on to love and good deeds.' In compiling this sports devotional, my fellow teammate and co-laborer in the gospel, Jill Ewert, is doing just that."

—*Kevin Hynes, University of Georgia Football Chaplain*

SHARING THE VICTORY
//BEING YOUR BEST *for* GOD

> > > > > > *by* **JILL EWERT**

summerside
PRESS

Summerside Press™
Minneapolis, MN 55337
www.summersidepress.com

SHARING THE VICTORY

Being Your Best for God
© 2011 by Jill Ewert

The title *Sharing the Victory* and magazine content are used with permission from the Fellowship of Christian Athletes.

ISBN 978-1-60936-203-4

Cover and interior design by Gearbox | studiogearbox.com.

Photo of Colt McCoy © John H. Reid III Photography;
Photo of Tamika Catchings © Pacers Sports & Entertainment;
Photo of Josh Hamilton © Brad Newton/Texas Rangers;
Background photo © iStockphoto.

Printed in China.

contents > >> > > > >> > >

foreword > > > > > > > >
by Sara Hall

A famous actor once said, "I think everybody should get rich and famous and do everything they ever dreamed of, so they can see that it's not the answer." After being in competitive running for more than half my life, I can agree with him in this, having experienced success and seen many dreams realized.

All of us are motivated by receiving love from others, and we too easily tie our performance to the reason why we are loved. But God's Word tells us we don't have to perform at all. We are so completely loved by Him that we can be free to compete, to take risks, to succeed, and to fail because, ultimately, it does not change His love for us one bit.

This is what being our best for God looks like: complete freedom knowing that the Father delights in watching us do our sports or our work to the best of our ability no matter what the outcome.

Just like the rest of the world, athletes must be very intentional about their heart condition. It takes the constant renewal of our minds and hearts to continue placing God on the throne of our lives, rather than assuming the position for ourselves. This doesn't mean it's never okay to have desires and goals for fear that they are selfish. God gives us desires and dreams for a reason, and He loves to collaborate with us to see them realized. The real issue is how we hold those desires in our hearts. Do they exist as idols that come before God? Or do we acknowledge them as gifts He's given us out of His love that are intended to point us back to loving Him?

God calls us to pursue excellence, but it's not about the end result, which is perfectionism. Instead, it's about the process of worshipping Him by being the very best version of who He created us to be. Though pursuing excellence is important, true freedom comes from realizing that, really, "it's not about you." But this is the exact opposite image of the typical bottom-of-the-ninth, bases-loaded mentality.

The pressure we put on ourselves, especially in sports, can be immense. But God never intended us to bear any burdens on our own. He gave us Jesus to bear all of our burdens on the cross. We get to do things like "play" sports in complete freedom knowing we are children who are fully loved and who cannot fail when our hearts are for God. Sure, we might miss our goal, but that isn't a failure because God causes all things to work together for our good (Romans 8:28). No matter what we do, we can't fail!

All aspects of life with Christ should be freeing, for "it is for freedom that Christ has set us free" (Galatians 5:1). Having this heart as a Christian should not mean we have one more set of expectations to live under or another standard to meet. I personally struggled with this for a long time and found it burdensome because, as hard as I tried, I never felt like I was competing with pure motives. I was still "performing" for Christ as if to gain His love and had forgotten that Jesus already paid the price. His righteousness was already covering me, and I no longer needed to perform. Because I am covered in that righteousness, God will never be disappointed in me, no matter what my heart is like.

Even if our hearts are sinful, according to Romans 2:4, His loving-kindness will lead us to repentance and change our heart's attitude. When we experience this love, it makes us want to be our best out of love for Him rather than by striving to do everything for ourselves or on our own.

To this day, God continues to renew my mind about these truths. As He does, I find that I get less nervous before competition; I enjoy it more and care less about the audience's perception of me, which frees me to take risks in my races knowing that I can't fail. As you read this devotional, I hope you let it renew your mind and realize that being your best for God brings you freedom to be the person He has created you to be—for both your enjoyment and His!

preface > >> > > > >> >

Being your best for God is a concept that has become very real to me over the last two years. It's a question that I've started to ask myself almost daily as I attempt to fulfill His calling on my life: *Am I truly being MY best for God?* Certainly there is a lot that goes into that question, and there is a lot that has gone behind it.

For years, I've struggled with being a Christian who has one eye on the Lord and one eye on the world. I've wanted so badly to please God but have also desired the approval of others—so much so that, two years ago, I wound up getting tangled in a mess of performance-driven athletic pursuits that caused some major destruction.

After college, I began working for the Fellowship of Christian Athletes with *Sharing the Victory* magazine. I'd been in or around sports all my life, so this was a natural fit for me and an amazing way to serve the Lord through my passion for sports. And it was during this time that I also picked up the new hobby of running.

I'd never been much of a runner, but when one of my buddies convinced me to do a local road race, I latched onto the sport like a leech.

For me, running was a way to feed my inner competitor. And, as I began to get more into it, I started to take it very seriously. I began pushing myself to always go farther and faster. It wasn't long before I'd tackled a half marathon and signed up for a full.

I trained hard and ran my first marathon in 2007. As soon as I crossed that finish line, before I even got back to my car, I'd already set a new goal. I wanted to qualify for the Boston Marathon—the only marathon in which you need to run a certain time in order to participate.

Without taking any time off, I jumped back into training and ran another marathon three months later. When I failed to qualify in that race, I signed up for another one four months later and trained again.

Finally, in that third marathon, I qualified. And that's when it all began to unravel.

In December, 2008, after completing marathon number four of the year (which I'd run just for fun) and just two weeks before the Boston training period began, I suffered an injury that took me completely out of the game. My body was so worn out and beat up from constant training that I developed a debilitating case of IT band syndrome in my left leg. So instead of training for the race I'd given up everything—relationships, health and time—to run, I spent the entire spring in physical rehab.

I was devastated. I cried often and unleashed many emotional outbursts on my friends and family. I couldn't understand why God would allow me to get so close to my dream only to take it away. Only now do I realize that God had to take running from me in order to teach me what it truly meant to run for Him.

During those months away from the road, He showed me that Boston—and really running itself—had become my god, my idol. And it was going to destroy me if it wasn't brought into a healthy balance.

Running is a fickle sport. Injuries are inevitable. Bodies are destructible. And there is always something more to achieve. If I would have continued letting myself get caught up in ever-higher goals, I would have missed out on much of the abundant life that God promised, as I would have been living in constant pursuit of the elusive "next best thing."

Through the loss of that dream, I realized that God Himself is the true "best thing." He is the only constant in life. When running left me, God did not. He was there through every rehab session, missed run, and tearful night reassuring me that His love for me wouldn't change regardless of whether or not I ever ran again.

Performance-driven self-worth is something we all battle, so it's important that we realize early that it's not a sentiment from God. He doesn't ask us to perform for Him. He doesn't ask us to earn His love. He simply asks that we do the best we can with what He's given us and allow Him to take care of the results.

Through my own journey, I came to the realization that God was wildly in love with me simply because I am His daughter, not because I could run a fast marathon. And, wouldn't you know it, once I'd surrendered my dream, He gave it right back to me. I was able to run the Boston Marathon just one year later, but with a totally different and liberated mindset.

The concept of being our best for God is something we need to embrace if we want to experience His true peace and joy. That's the whole point of this book. Through the examples of athletes and coaches who understand and who have gone through similar struggles, we can learn how to focus on our Father instead of on worldly results. We can learn what it means to be the best version of ourselves as He created us to be—not the world's best, but God's best. And I am fully convinced that's all He wants.

–Jill Ewert

acknowledgments

Special thanks to the following:

The wonderful athletes and coaches who trusted me with their faith stories. Their fantastic agents, media relations teams, and PR reps.

Everyone who endorsed this book and was brave enough to lend their names and support.

The fantastic Sara Hall—both a marvelous writer and runner.

Ken Williams, Tom Rogeberg, Dan Britton, Ashley Burns, Clay Meyer, Nancy Hedrick, and the staff at the FCA National Support Center, as well as my extended FCA family across the country.

The wonderful folks at Summerside Press, especially Marilyn, Joanie, Jason, and Carlton.

My home team: Momsy, PPB, Jamus ("editor-in-chief"), Topher, Jackie, Jim and Georgia, Jessi, Erin, AMac, ANew, Janice, my church family, and maybe every English teacher/journalism professor I ever had.

And, above all, my Father. What a gift.

Do your best to present yourself to God as one approved, a worker who does not need to be ashamed and who correctly handles the word of truth. *—2 Timothy 2:15*

being your best for God//

humility

> > > > > > > >

 Humility: the quality or state of being humble; not proud or haughty; not arrogant or assertive

Sitting down, Jesus called the Twelve and said, "If anyone wants to be first, he must be last of all, and servant of all." —Mark 9:35 hcsb

I run in the path of your commands, for you have broadened my understanding. —Psalm 119:32

NAME: Ryan Hall

SPORT: Professional Distance Runner

HIGHLIGHTS: 2010 Olympian;
American record holder in the half marathon
Fastest U.S.-born men's marathon runner

California was just about the last place he wanted to be at that moment. Instead of racing through the streets of Athens as the Olympian he believed himself to be, Stanford University distance runner Ryan Hall was sitting at home eating chips and salsa and watching the race on TV.

Competing in the Olympics had been his dream ever since he'd taken his first fifteen-mile run around California's Big Bear Lake with his dad. A teenager at the time, he'd longed to feel the gold medal around his neck and hear "The Star-Spangled Banner" as he stood atop the podium. But there he sat: burned out, frustrated, and heartbroken.

The trouble for Hall wasn't physical; it was spiritual. The Olympics—in fact, the sport of running itself—had become so all-consuming to him that it had become an idol. He lived, ate, breathed, and moved to run and to win. Hall had been a Christian most of his life, but, in his heart, the Lord was a second-place finisher to his sport.

"I could sum it up in one word," Hall said. "Obsession."

Most of us can identify with Ryan Hall. When competing, we easily slip into a performance-driven mentality that thrives on setting and achieving goals. Often, if we're not careful, those goals overtake us and we become consumed by them, rewiring our entire lives to pursue an achievement, championship, or record. The goal or sport becomes our ultimate source of meaning and the basis for our happiness.

When we find ourselves in this frame of mind, we are, in fact, caught in idolatry. We worship the finish. We bow down to the clock. We revere the trophy, the title, the prestige, the accomplishment. Somewhere in the back of our minds we think achievement will bring us the happiness and value that nothing else can—not even God.

"I'm now free to run, which means not carrying the burdens of this world."

When we allow ourselves to be consumed by a goal or a sport, we essentially tell God that He alone cannot meet our needs and that something apart from Him will provide fulfillment. Either directly or indirectly, we communicate that Christ's sacrifice and love aren't enough to make us whole; we need applause and honor for that.

Through God's grace, however, we all eventually find out that this is a lie. If we achieve a goal, we discover that it doesn't provide the lasting happiness we thought it would. In fact, it usually just makes us want to achieve more. After all, winning means having to defend the win. So does breaking a record. And if we earn one MVP award, we immediately start calculating how many we'll need in order to be named the all-time greatest.

Idols are merciless. They require constant feeding and constant worship. There will always be something higher, bigger, better, stronger, or faster. Making any kind of achievement our sole purpose will eventually drive us crazy or kill us. It won't prove fulfilling or peaceful like we once thought it would, and it certainly won't bring the love we seek through its attention.

But the good news for performance-junkies is that we don't have to worship an accomplishment or sport to find what we're looking for. We have a God who loves us—end of story. We don't have to win any title or break any record to earn it. All He asks is that we receive His love and do the best we can with what He's given us. That is what He considers true victory.

Ryan Hall discovered this truth. During his brokenness, he realized his own idolatry and confessed it to the Lord. He received God's love for who he was as His child and found freedom to run with passion again—and purpose. And when he finally took to the streets of Beijing in the 2008 Summer Olympics, he did so with an understanding that he was running for the Lord and not the clock.

"I'm now free to run, which means not carrying the burdens of this world," Hall said. "It's the freedom to not have to achieve something—to be able to just go out and do it for the love of doing it. To do it because I feel like God created me to do it and to run as an act of worship to God."

Today, if you are enslaved to an achievement idol, ask the Lord to help you get free. Accept His unconditional love for you, which has nothing to do with your performance and everything to do with the fact that you are His child. Be your best for Him by laying that idol at His feet and asking Him to renew your mind. Once you do, like Ryan Hall, you will be "free to run" for Him.

> Your Turn

To what extent are you driven by performance? _____

_____

_____

_____

How much of your personal value do you base on achievement?

_____

_____

_____

What does it mean to be "free to run"? _____

_____

_____

_____

What is keeping you from that freedom? _____

_____

_____

_____

> **Being Your Best for God:**
> **Run from idolatry.**

enjoy the
game

*Rejoice in the Lord always. I will say it
again: Rejoice!* —Philippians 4:4

NAME: Cam Ward

TEAM: Carolina Hurricanes

POSITION: Goalie

HIGHLIGHTS: 2006 Stanley Cup Champion
2011 NHL All-Star

Why is it so rare to see athletes smiling during competition? Is it because they're intense and aggressive, completely focused on the game? Or is it because they believe that if they're having fun they're not taking the game seriously? Both can be the case when it comes to "serious" competition, but what if it didn't have to be this way?

People often think smiling or laughing is a sign of irresponsibility. While this can be true at times, many of us have adopted it as a hard-and-fast rule. We think that if we are enjoying ourselves, we're not taking our sport or our job seriously. But some, including NHL goalie Cam Ward, think competition can be both fun and competitive.

"When I grew up, my dad always told me that the more fun you have, the better you do, and I strongly believe that," said Ward, a longtime Christian who, in 2006, became the first rookie goalie to win a Stanley Cup. "In my position in the NHL, there is pressure, but I still make sure that every time I come to the rink, I come to have some fun. And I find that's when I play my best."

Whether or not Ward is actually smiling while he's on the ice is hard to tell considering that his face is hidden by protective plastic. But would it be such a bad thing if he was? By his own admonition, he competes at his best when he's enjoying the game, and he's comfortable expressing that as he guards the net.

Believe it or not, being your best for God involves joy. Sports weren't intended to be torture devices or pressure vacuums. Yes, there are times when we should have our game faces on, and, if smiles and laughter are rooted in irresponsibility we need to read Colossians 3:23. But if we take a look at God's Word, we will find that His plan for our lives includes joy in every area—including competition.

> "In my position in the NHL, there is pressure, but I still make sure that every time I come to the rink, I come to have some fun. And I find that's when I play my best."

In Philippians 4:4, the apostle Paul tells us, "Rejoice in the Lord always. I will say it again: Rejoice!" Notice the word "always." It's a clear time frame that includes every moment of our day, including the time we spend on the court or field. In fact, it even covers those grueling two-a-day preseason practices.

But what does it look like to actually enjoy something that is physically or mentally demanding? How do we access the joy of the Lord when we're down by two in the final minutes of a game? The answer is by trusting God with the outcome. Knowing and believing that He is in control and that He has our best interests in mind releases us from the pressure of living up to expectations. Once that pressure is off, we're free to enjoy the experience no matter how intense it is.

By all means, we should focus and compete with intensity and effort. The Lord's desire is that we do all things to the best of the ability He's given us. But we need to do so with the understanding that He loves us in both failure and success. Once we understand this truth, we will be able to enjoy even the most adrenaline-filled moment knowing that He is right there with us.

Take a lesson from Cam Ward, and next time you compete, ask yourself if you are having fun and enjoying yourself. If God gave you the ability and desire, then He assuredly wants to bless you through the experience (Romans 8:28). Why not take Him at His Word and have a little fun?

Your Turn

Do you think athletes should ever smile on the field? Why or why not? _____

_____

_____

_____

Under what circumstances is it okay to smile or laugh

in competition? _____

_____

_____

_____

What's keeping you from experiencing the joy of the Lord while

working hard? _____

_____

_____

_____

Being Your Best for God:
Win or lose, enjoy the game!

victory
in defeat

"For my thoughts are not your thoughts, neither are your ways my ways," declares the Lord. "As the heavens are higher than the earth, so are my ways higher than your ways and my thoughts than your thoughts." —Isaiah 55:8–9

NAME: Colt McCoy

TEAM: Cleveland Browns

POSITION: Quarterback

HIGHLIGHTS: Heisman Trophy runner-up (2008)
First Team NCAA All-American (2009)

As a senior at the University of Texas, NFL quarterback Colt McCoy had hoped for a national title to cap off his honor-laden college career. After the final whistle blew on McCoy's Longhorn reign, however, he found himself standing injured and heartbroken on the opposite end of the celebration, fielding questions about what it was like to experience a crushing loss.

After being slammed to the turf early in the first quarter of the 2009 BCS National Championship game, McCoy had injured his passing shoulder and been forced to the sidelines, unable to even compete in his final collegiate game. He had to watch helplessly as the team he'd led for four years battled through the biggest game of their lives without him, eventually falling to the Alabama Crimson Tide 37–21.

That night, however, McCoy proved that sometimes the greatest victories are achieved in defeat. The picture of both sorrow and peace, the battered quarterback stood bravely in front of the TV cameras during the post-game interview and proclaimed, "I never ask why. God is in control of my life, and I'm standing on the Rock."

Being raised in a Christian home and learning to live for Christ as a young man, McCoy had earned a reputation of faith during his rise to fame as a Texas Longhorn. As his national recognition grew, McCoy continually acknowledged that his position was about more than just football.

"I realized God gave me the opportunity and that it's a platform to shine the light for Him," McCoy said. "I wouldn't be here without Him, and I want people to be able to see Christ shining through me."

Mission accomplished. By trusting the Lord in what can only be described as a worst-case athletic scenario, McCoy displayed the kind of peace that can only be found through faith in Jesus Christ. His words revealed that his God wasn't a football trophy, but that it was, and is, the Lord Almighty who loved McCoy regardless of what happened on the field.

The picture of both sorrow and peace, the battered quarterback stood bravely in front of the TV cameras during the post-game interview and proclaimed, "I never ask why. God is in control of my life, and I'm standing on the Rock."

Isaiah 55:8–9 offers a powerful statement from God, stating, "'For my thoughts are not your thoughts, neither are your ways my ways,' declares the Lord. 'As the heavens are higher than the earth, so are my ways higher than your ways and my thoughts than your thoughts.'"

In sports—and in life—things often don't turn out like we plan. No one walks onto an athletic field hoping to get beat, but it happens. No one wants to experience pain, yet it's inevitable. But in disappointing situations we often find we can stand taller for the Lord than if we had achieved success.

Because no one expects a defeated athlete to have a peaceful perspective, people take notice when one does. And when that athlete acknowledges Christ as the source of all peace, others witness the power of God. Seeing that strength in hardship, they begin to desire it for themselves.

Consider how much different McCoy's situation would have been if he and the Longhorns had won the game. If he had praised God for helping them win, his words would have been chalked up as typical post-game comments—the kind made by any number of athletes who feel blessed by a title. But by making the same statement with a broken heart, McCoy demonstrated a faith more real than most viewers had ever seen. And only God knows how their hearts were changed as they reflected on the quarterback's unshakable faith.

Part of being your best for God involves learning to praise Him in disappointment. No one goes undefeated for life. So when your turn comes, recognize it as a divine opportunity to display the peace you have through faith in Christ. Follow in Colt McCoy's footsteps and leave a legacy of faith and peace more powerful than any final score.

Your Turn

Imagine yourself in Colt McCoy's situation. How would you have responded? _____

_____

_____

Have you ever questioned God's goodness after a loss or injury?

Explain. _____

_____

_____

Are you questioning it now? Why? _____

_____

_____

How can praising God in defeat be a more powerful witness than

praising Him in victory? _____

_____

_____

Are you prepared to praise Him in both? _____

_____

_____

Being Your Best for God:
Be a winner even when you lose.

mr. nice guy

Therefore, as God's chosen people, holy and dearly loved, clothe yourselves with compassion, kindness, humility, gentleness and patience.... And over all these virtues put on love, which binds them all together in perfect unity. —Colossians 3:12, 14

NAME: Mike Sweeney

TEAMS: Kansas City Royals
Oakland Athletics
Seattle Mariners
Philadelphia Phillies

POSITION: First Base

HIGHLIGHTS: Five-time MLB All-Star (2000–2003, 2005)

When it comes to legacies, most of us want to leave a lasting impression of greatness. We want to break records, make history, and be remembered for doing what no one else could. And, for most, the best way to do that is through scoreboards, bottom lines, or titles.

There are a certain few, however, who believe that true greatness is achieved not by being the best statistically, but by being the best child of God they can be. They believe God called them to the "mission field" of athletics in order to share His love and truth with those around them and those watching from the stands.

One of those "missionaries" is Mike Sweeney, a five-time MLB All-Star and respected American League slugger. More than that, though, he is one of the nicest guys in sports.

Raised in a Christian home, Sweeney grew up understanding that his role was to live for Christ. Then, while making his way through the minor leagues, the young slugger fully surrendered his life to Christ as Lord and embraced his spiritual calling of sharing Him with others.

"I want to take as many of my teammates and my family members to heaven with me as I can, and Christ is the only way there," Sweeney said. "St. Francis of Assisi said we should preach the gospel at all times, and, if necessary use words. That's what I try to do."

It seems that no one has a bad thing to say about Mike Sweeney. His reputation among teammates, coaches, and fans is so positive that, in 2003 and 2004, he was officially given the Good

Guy in Sports title by *The Sporting News* and named by peers as the "Nicest Guy in Baseball."

When reading those labels, we may be tempted to think: *Nice? Doesn't that mean he's soft and passive?* Most of us don't pursue the goal of being known as "nice" because it conflicts with our ability to be tough and competitive.

Somewhere along the line, the word "nice" got confused with being mild-mannered and weak. And when it comes to competition, whether in life or in sports, those aren't adjectives we want attached to our names. But understanding what the word really means might change our minds.

The definition for "nice" includes the powerful synonyms "courteous" and "of good character"—two traits that are far from passive or weak. In fact, living with courtesy and good character takes a tremendous amount of courage and effort.

> "I want to take as many of my teammates and my family members to heaven with me as I can, and Christ is the only way there."

Think of the last time you had to force yourself to be kind to someone who didn't deserve it. Maybe someone shoved you and tried to coax you into a fight. The easy thing to do in that situation would be to push back and let emotions take over. The harder thing would be to respond calmly and let Christ help you control your anger.

Based on its true definition, being nice has little to do with being soft and everything to do with being strong enough to love others when it's hard: being strong enough to be kind when others don't deserve it; strong enough to take the high road in situations when it would be so easy to let go of our convictions; strong enough to exhibit the character of Christ in any and every situation. It's one of the hardest things to do in life, but it's one of the most rewarding. When we exhibit the kindness of Christ, we inevitably become magnets for those around us who are desperately in need of His love. It gives us the opportunity to lead them into a relationship with Him.

Mike Sweeney gets it. He embraces being nice and pursues it because he knows it has a powerful impact. He's not passive on the field, nor is he a pushover off of it. He is, however, regarded as one of the most loving and caring players the game has ever known.

Today, be your best for God simply by being nice. When you do, you will build a legacy that extends beyond the field and echoes into eternity.

Your Turn

How would you define the word "nice"?

_____

_____

_____

Do you think of it as positive or negative in competition? Why?

_____

_____

_____

_____

What gave you the impression you have? _____

_____

_____

_____

What does God say about the importance of good character?

_____

_____

_____

How can having good character lead others to Christ? _____

_____

_____

_____

Being Your Best for God:
Nice guys finish first.

all about enthusiasm

*Clap your hands, all you nations; shout to
God with cries of joy.* —Psalm 47:1

NAME: Anthony Parker

TEAM: Cleveland Cavaliers

POSITION: Guard

HIGHLIGHTS: Two-time Euroleague MVP (2005, 2006)
Euroleague 2001–2010 All-Decade Team
Post-season NBA appearances with both the
Toronto Raptors and Cleveland Cavaliers

He had just finished up a playoff run with the Toronto Raptors, but that didn't matter to NBA guard Anthony Parker. His time off could wait. There was important business to tend to—business that involved games of H-O-R-S-E, cafeteria meals, and spirit sticks.

Yes, spirit sticks—as in cheerleading spirit sticks.

It was 2008, and a local Fellowship of Christian Athletes summer camp was in full swing in Springfield, Illinois, home of Parker's alma mater Bradley University. Just like they did every day at the end of camp, the kids were voting for who they thought displayed the highest level of enthusiasm and, that day, Parker was their man. Among cheers and hollers from adoring junior-high athletes, Parker graciously accepted the spirit stick as his reward, thanked the audience, and then went back to embracing his fun-loving, inner thirteen-year-old. He was truly one of them, and they loved him for it.

"I loved being at camp with those kids," Parker said. "A lot of kids don't get to see that side of professional athletics, so it was a great opportunity for me to share my faith with them and to show them a little fun and enthusiasm while I was at it."

Talk about making a difference. The kids at that camp will never forget Anthony Parker. He was an NBA star, but he didn't act like it. He was more of a big brother to them than a celebrity, and his love for each camper was clearly communicated through joyful interaction.

"I just want to help bring as many to Christ as I can," Parker said, "and enthusiasm is a great way to communicate Him."

There's a popular phrase in sports that says nothing great was ever achieved without enthusiasm, which comes very close to words written by the apostle Paul. In Colossians 3:23, Paul wrote, "Whatever you do, do it enthusiastically, as something done for the Lord and not for men." Through the high-fives and pats on the back he gave out at the FCA camp, Anthony Parker embodied this verse and left lasting imprints on the hearts of young athletes.

We all dream of having teammates like Parker—the kind who lift us up when things get intense and who encourage us to keep going. They are the ones who always have a positive attitude when practice gets long, repetition gets boring, and workouts get exhausting. Teammates and friends like that are irreplaceable.

Enthusiasm is important for many reasons. One is because God asks us to display it. But it's not an instruction He gave without purpose. He knows that when we choose to be enthusiastic about a task, it reveals specific characteristics about Christ and His followers. Enthusiasm displays the joy He has given through the Holy Spirit, who places peace and gladness in our hearts the moment we receive Christ as Lord (Galatians 5:22).

Another benefit of enthusiasm is that it tells the world that we as Christians don't live in fear. Consistent joy reveals to others that we don't base our value in a victory but in our identity as beloved children of God. Thus, we don't fear losing because we know we are valued by Him regardless of the outcome. We're free to be at peace and do our best for Him knowing that He will take care of the results and love us no matter what.

Finally, enthusiasm is also a great way to love others. As Christians, we have the unique opportunity to convey Christ's love to those who are closest to us. Because we are around them in a variety of situations, we can communicate His love to them on a regular basis through both actions and words. And enthusiasm is a great way to deliver it. Our joy lifts the spirits of our teammates, friends, or coworkers, bringing them hope even in despair, which is most certainly an act of Christ-like love.

> "I just want to help bring as many to Christ as I can, and enthusiasm is a great way to communicate Him."

Today, if you want to be your best for God, don't just go through the routine without emotion. Like Anthony Parker, embrace the opportunity to enthusiastically engage with those around you. As the Lord's child, you know that you are forgiven and free and that your value isn't determined by a scoreboard. Why not use the resulting joy to reveal Christ to others? Who knows—you might just win a spiritual spirit stick of your own.

Your Turn

How would you rate your level of enthusiasm? _____

_____

_____

How does it affect you when a teammate or friend displays

enthusiasm during a tough moment? _____

_____

_____

How does enthusiasm reflect the character of Christ? _____

_____

_____

What are some ways you can show more enthusiasm on and off

the court? _____

_____

_____

Being Your Best for God:
Achieve great things with enthusiasm!

humble
hero

Do nothing out of selfish ambition or vain conceit.
Rather, in humility value others above yourselves,
not looking to your own interests but each of you to
the interests of the others. —Philippians 2:3–4

NAME: Albert Pujols

TEAM: St. Louis Cardinals

POSITION: First Base

HIGHLIGHTS: Nine-time MLB All-Star (2001, 2003–2010)
2006 World Series Champion
Three-time NL MVP

If anyone could justify being prideful based on athletic ability, it would be Albert Pujols. After being named Rookie of the Year in 2001, Pujols began dominating Major League Baseball and never looked back. By the time he was thirty, he had already been selected to nine All-Star games, crowned the NL MVP three times, named the baseball player of the decade by *The Sporting News* and captured a World Series title with the St. Louis Cardinals.

Big stats. Big awards. Big head, right? Not in this case. As a Christian, Pujols is known as much for his faith and humility as he is for his heavy bat.

Case in point: In 2005 Pujols and his wife, Deidre, established the Pujols Family Foundation—an organization that would, in part, focus on bringing aid and medical relief to the impoverished people of the Dominican Republic, the country where Pujols was born. Through the foundation, he and Deidre, along with a team of volunteers, still make annual trips to the Dominican in order to meet specific medical needs of the locals.

As a sports icon, Pujols could choose to relax and take life easy. He has everything the world considers desirable including fame, family, money, and talent. But instead of being content with the world's idea of "having it all," this All-Star slugger would rather spend his off seasons helping underprivileged children read eye charts than lounging by a pool.

But why? What's the point?

"Everybody thinks my job is playing baseball, but it's not; that's the platform God has given me," Pujols said. "My job is to be obedient to God and do the things He wants me to do for His will."

Albert Pujols gets what it means to be his best for God. It's not about him; it's about Jesus Christ.

"The Lord has blessed me with the ability to play sports and given me a platform," he said. "He could have chosen anyone else, but He chose me. So, I want to make sure I do His will and do it the right way."

> "My job is to be obedient to God and do the things He wants me to do for His will."

While the sports community may value a sixty home run season and big paychecks, God values things that last—things like love, mercy, and serving. And what is important to God is important to His children, Pujols included. Those who truly love Jesus will value what He values regardless of the world's opinion.

It's easy to allow pride to take root in our hearts. When we achieve a little success, we start to walk a little taller, hold our heads a little higher, and talk a little louder. We start to view people differently and entertain thoughts of how much better we are by comparison. We treat others with less respect and treat ourselves to more of what we think we deserve based on what we can do.

In Mark 9:35, however, Jesus tells His disciples, "If anyone wants to be first, he must be last of all and the servant of all." What a counter-cultural statement! According to Christ, the true big-timers of the world are the ones who put others before themselves and faithfully serve Him with a humble and submitted heart. The "first" are the ones who climb down from their pedestals and get dirty with those in need. They believe that, as children of God, everyone is on a level playing field and that, according to God's truth, none of us is anything more than a mere sinner in need of a Savior. No one person is better than another regardless of bank account, social status, or batting average.

When it comes to what really counts in the eyes of God, stats matter exactly none. That's why Albert Pujols doesn't think he's too big-time to serve others. His batting average doesn't make him any better in God's economy than less-prolific teammates or those who never make it out of the minors. The world may take notice of his records, but they don't matter as much to Pujols himself. He serves an Audience of One and buys into a different system—one in which the bat boy is more of an All-Star than the slugger.

Today, refuse to embrace the world's mindset regarding fame and fortune. Instead, be your best for God by loving and serving others. In the end, those are the only stats that truly matter.

Your Turn

What situations generate pride in your heart? _____

_____

_____

_____

What damage does pride do to your relationship with God? _____

_____

_____

_____

What does it mean that the last shall be first? How does that

apply to both sports and life? _____

_____

_____

What is one way you can serve your teammates and peers? _____

_____

_____

_____

Being Your Best for God:
True all-stars put others first.

> > > > > > > > > > > > > >

being your best for God//

faith

> >   >   >   > >   >   >

 Faith: belief and trust in and loyalty to God;
complete trust

*Now faith is confidence in what we hope for and
assurance about what we do not see.*   —Hebrews 11:1

wisdom
on the run

*Do you not know that your bodies are temples of the Holy
Spirit, who is in you, whom you have received from God?
You are not your own; you were bought at a price. Therefore
honor God with your bodies.* —1 Corinthians 6:19–20

NAME: Catherine Ndereba

SPORT: Professional Distance Runner

HIGHLIGHTS: Four-time Boston Marathon winner
Two-time Olympic silver medalist
Former women's marathon world record holder

She's been called the greatest female marathoner of all time—an impressive title in a sport that has been around since 490 BC. But with four Boston Marathon victories, two Olympic medals, two World Championship titles, and a marathon personal record of 2:18:47, it's hard to disagree.

Her name is Catherine Ndereba, a.k.a. Catherine the Great.

After beginning her international racing career in 1995, Ndereba made her marathon debut in 1998 and soon skyrocketed to elite status by winning back-to-back Boston and Chicago marathons in 2000 and 2001, even setting a new world record in her second Chicago victory.

Over the years, Ndereba continued her racing success and was scheduled to return to Boston in 2010. As usual, she trained hard for the event and hoped to return to victory, but just ten days before the race, she was forced to withdraw due to a muscle tear. Doctors said that, while she could have run, the damage to her body would have been severe. As a result, Ndereba pulled out of the marathon in order to race well another day.

"It was hard to make the decision not to run," she told the audience at the Fellowship of Christian Athletes pre-race chapel service in Boston, "but I know it's the right thing to do."

With her decision, Ndereba chose to set aside her own agenda in order to exercise wisdom and self-discipline, which is rarely an easy thing to do. We often get so focused on personal goals that when something unexpected comes up, like an injury, we wind up being foolish with our bodies. Cortisone shots, pain killers, prescription medications—all are temporary Band-Aids that mask serious problems in need of correction. While these treatments have their places, they are frequently misused when common, everyday wisdom and patience would be the better treatment.

"In the Christian life, if we don't sacrifice, we won't be able to overcome," Ndereba said. "It was a difficult decision, but I know that the Lord has a greater plan."

When it comes to being our best for God, wisdom and good judgment are essential. In 1 Corinthians 6:19–20, the apostle Paul writes, "Do you not know that your bodies are temples of the Holy Spirit, who is in you, whom you have received from God? You are not your own; you were bought at a price. Therefore honor God with your bodies."

Athletes are tough, and that's a good thing. Our determination and focus can lead to great displays of physical power and skill that can bring glory to the Lord. However, when our personal agendas take us to the point of destroying the temple of God's Holy Spirit—our bodies—we actually discredit the very witness we've tried so hard to maintain. Through our driven actions, we tell the world that success matters more than anything else in life and that we lack the self-control *not* to compete. We are controlled by a sport (or a career), and we base our identity on being performance-driven instead of being children of God.

Somewhere along the line we bought into the misconception that our value is connected to our achievements, and that lie is what has driven us to keep pushing beyond what is wise. *The pain in my hamstring is killing me, but if I sit out, people will think I'm weak.... If I somehow play on this sprained ankle, I will finally prove to the coach that I'm tough and can play through anything....*

"In the Christian life, if we don't sacrifice, we won't be able to overcome."

Certainly there are times when pressing on in spite of pain can glorify God, but if our motives are rooted in a mistaken identity or in lies from the enemy, it isn't likely that God is the one asking us to keep powering through. That's why, in each situation, it's important to ask ourselves whether we are being propelled by God or driven by pride or insecurity. The answer to that will help determine His will. And if we truly understand that He loves us regardless of our performance, we will be able to rest in whatever decision He gives, knowing that He has a good plan for both the current situation and the future.

Through her own injury, Catherine Ndereba was able to exercise wisdom, and because she did, was able to recover without causing unnecessary damage to her body. If the greatest female marathoner of all time can trust the Lord and be at peace with letting one race go by, it's safe to say you can do the same. It's just part of being your best for God.

Have you ever exercised or performed through physical pain when you shouldn't have? What were the results? _____

_____

_____

_____

Why did you feel the need to push your body? _____

_____

_____

_____

What is the difference between being compelled by God and driven by pride? Are you able to discern the difference in your life? _____

_____

_____

_____

Being Your Best for God:
Don't play through pain out of pride.

trust God —period

Trust in the Lord with all your heart and lean not on your own understanding. —Proverbs 3:5

NAME: Ernie Johnson

CAREER: On-air sports broadcaster

SPORTS: NBA, MLB, NFL, NCAA, Olympic Games

Just like the athletes he covers, sportscaster Ernie Johnson has had to deal with tough opponents throughout his career. As the man who sits between Charles Barkley and Kenny Smith in his role as studio host for the NBA on TNT, Johnson has had to hold his own with some big personalities. In 2003, however, Johnson met an opponent that made even Barkley seem like a pushover. The opponent was cancer.

While he might not have realized it at the time of his diagnosis, Johnson was equipped for the battle. It wasn't because he had a specific set of self-cultivated personality traits or could afford great doctors. Cancer outmatched even those. Only one thing gave Johnson the strength he needed to endure the challenge, and that was his faith in Jesus Christ.

"When people have asked me how I got through it, I tell them the three words I lived by: 'Trust God. Period,'" Johnson said. "Since I came to Jesus, my life is no longer me-centered, but Christ-centered. I look at my life now and what I've been through, and I praise God because, even if I can't see it, I know He's got a plan for my life."

Johnson's motto is to trust God—period. End of story. Not trust God *if* this or *when* that, but trust Him *period*. Because he knew that the Lord was constantly with him every time he felt sick, every time he lost another strand of hair, every second he was afraid, Johnson could trust that he was in good hands.

Just like Johnson, we all have the ability to choose faith when facing difficult situations. No matter what challenges arise, we can decide to believe that the Lord our God is faithful.

In His Word, God reminds us repeatedly that He is trustworthy. He gives us promises such as, "Never will I leave you, never will I forsake you" (Hebrews 13:5). "For I know the plans I have for you... plans to prosper you and not to harm you. Plans to give you a hope and a future" (Jeremiah 29:11). "And we know that in all things, God works for the good of those who love Him who have been called according to his purpose" (Romans 8:28).

> "I look at my life now and what I've been through, and I praise God because, even if I can't see it, I know He's got a plan for my life."

For those of us who believe that God's Word is the truth, these verses allow us to start each day knowing that He is at work on our behalf in any and every situation. As the day progresses, we can encounter each new obstacle with peace and handle it without fear because we know that, in spite of what it may seem, God has a perfect plan. It may not be what we would have chosen or desired, but we can trust that He will bless us through the circumstance by revealing Himself and drawing us closer to Him.

But we don't have to wait for major obstacles like cancer to practice trusting God. This principle applies to every situation from having a bad game to getting stuck in a traffic jam.

Every day, we face situations that can cause us to doubt God's love. According to John 8:32, if we know God's truth—which includes details about His trustworthy character—it will make us free. And that freedom includes liberation from fear and anxiety. When we know who He is, we can let go of our worries, trust Him, and embrace His peace.

Part of being your best for God will involve facing challenges—both big and small—with the kind of faith that trusts Him implicitly. When you do, you'll be able to rejoice when He delivers on His promises, knowing that you didn't lose a single minute on worry. Like Ernie Johnson, you can simply trust God—period—and let Him take care of the rest.

Your Turn

What situations make it most difficult for you to trust God? _____

_____

_____

_____

In those times, what makes you doubt His faithfulness? _____

_____

_____

_____

Do you believe that His Word is true? Why or why not? _____

_____

_____

_____

How can trusting God be a powerful witness to others? _____

_____

_____

_____

Being Your Best for God:
Trust God with every opponent.

just an
at-bat

*See what great love the Father has lavished on
us, that we should be called children of God!
And that is what we are!* —1 John 3:1

NAME: Jamey Carroll

TEAM: Los Angeles Dodgers

POSITION: Infielder

HIGHLIGHTS: 2010 Roy Campanella Award winner
2006 MLB fielding percentage leader (second base)

Major league infielder Jamey Carroll has a history of coming through in high-pressure situations. After making his big-league debut in 2002, Carroll quickly earned a reputation for confidence on the field based on a handful of revealing stats that included a 2005 batting average that was at its highest when Carroll was at the plate with runners in scoring position with two outs.

The key to Carroll's success in high-pressure situations?

"Basically, I realize that I have nothing to lose," he said. "My former first-base coach told me that when he'd go to the plate he'd say, 'God loves me, my family loves me, and it's just an at-bat.' Having that mindset really helped me."

It's a mantra that has served Carroll well as he's put his stamp on Major League Baseball—a career that included a World Series appearance in 2007 with the Colorado Rockies.

"I just try to let everything go and know that God is in my corner," Carroll said. "I've prepared what I can, so I can just go out and play ball."

The pressure to perform is one of the most common obstacles we face in being our best for God. We step up to the plate and immediately become aware of the number of eyes on us. Our stomachs tighten; our pulse speeds up. We think, *What if I swing and miss? I'll look ridiculous, and I'll let everyone down. I have to prove that I can come through in the clutch.*

It is similar in every sport. Volleyball players walk slowly back to the serving line thinking, *I can't hit it into the net or serve it out of bounds. My team needs this.* Basketball players feel it at the free-throw line; track runners at the starting blocks. Any kind of career involves high-pressure situations in which the collective stare of the audience is focused solely on a single person. It just comes with the territory.

While we may dread these intense moments, God actually delights in them. Whether we realize it or not, these are the times in which He waits to meet us in powerful ways. In fact, He sets up these moments in order to teach us more about Himself by proving Himself faithful—no matter what.

Jamey Carroll's coach was onto something with the statement, "God loves me.… It's just an at-bat."

In those times when we feel so squeezed we think we're going to crack under the pressure, we need to realize that there are things going on in the spiritual realm we can't see. While our human eyes focus on the physical dynamics of the game around us, God is zeroing in on our hearts. He wants to teach us to trust Him more deeply, knowing that, when the moment is over—whether we hit a home run or struck out looking—He loves us just the same.

If we embrace that love and allow ourselves to experience it in those moments, we will be taken to a deeper level of faith. We'll understand more fully just how little our true worth and value have to do with a stat sheet. We will know in our souls that we are more important to God than how we appear on paper.

Take a look at Romans 8:38–39: "For I am convinced that neither death nor life, neither angels nor demons, neither the present nor the future, nor any powers, neither height nor depth, nor anything else in all creation, will be able to separate us from the love of God that is in Christ Jesus our Lord." Somewhere in between the present, future, and "anything else in all creation" lay the strikeouts, missed opportunities, and fumbles. That kind of love and acceptance isn't something that can be found in the world around us.

> "I just try to let everything go and know that God is in my corner. I've prepared what I can, so I can just go out and play ball."

If we swing and miss, the world turns on us by telling us we're not good enough— that we're less important than the person who could have hit that curveball. But that is the opinion of a broken belief system from people who are lost and searching for meaning. And, if we're not careful, we'll believe that lie every time.

If, however, we are rooted in Scripture and know what God says about us—that He loved us so much that He sacrificed His own Son, Jesus Christ, on our behalf—we can walk away from those situations, regardless of the outcome, and know that He is still pleased with us simply because we are His children.

Truly being your best for God means being able to let go of pressure in the most intense moments and realize that you are eternally valued and loved by your Father in heaven. Whatever your case may be, you can take a page from Jamey Carroll's book and always remember one thing: God loves you, and it's just an at-bat.

Your Turn

How do you handle high-pressure situations? _____

_____

_____

What is your biggest fear in those moments? _____

_____

_____

What's the worst thing that would happen if your fears came

true? Would your value change in God's eyes? _____

_____

_____

What can you do to remember His love for you next time you're in

a high-pressure situation? _____

_____

_____

Being Your Best for God:
Handle high pressure with a High Power.

faith in the future

"For I know the plans I have for you," declares the Lord, "plans to prosper you and not to harm you, plans to give you hope and a future." —Jeremiah 29:11

NAME: Charlotte Smith

CURRENT TEAM: University of North Carolina, Assistant Women's Basketball Coach

WNBA CAREER: Charlotte Sting
Washington Mystics

COLLEGE CAREER: 1995 First-Team All-American (UNC)

Fear of the future is something we all experience. It doesn't matter if we're professional athletes or average joes, we all deal with anxiety about what's ahead.

"That's one of the things I worry about the most," said former WNBA All-Star Charlotte Smith, who joined the coaching staff at the University of North Carolina after retiring from her ESPY-Award winning pro career. "We can become so anxious to know what is in store for us and God's plans for our lives that, when it's not unfolding and we're walking in the dark, we start to worry."

It may be surprising to learn that an outstanding athlete and coach like Smith battles anxiety about the future, but she is human. And, just like you and me, she can't see beyond the current moment.

Our limited vision often causes us to worry. We spend hours making plans and preparing for what we think might happen tomorrow, next week, or next year. While it's not a bad thing to plan ahead, it can become a harmful distraction if we allow it to lead to anxiety or fear. When a simple question like, *Will I be noticed by the college scouts?* becomes, *What if I don't get a scholarship offer and don't meet the expectations of everyone around me?* there is a problem.

The good news is that God understands our battle. That's why over and over in Scripture He tells us to trust Him and not to worry. It's one thing Jesus addressed by telling His followers repeatedly not to be afraid. In verses such as the often-quoted John 14:27, He says, "Peace I leave with you; my peace I give you. I do not give to you as the world gives. Do not let your hearts be troubled and do not be afraid."

> **"We can become so anxious to know what is in store for us and God's plans for our lives that, when it is not unfolding and we're walking in the dark, we start to worry."**

Jesus knew that His Father had a plan in place for every one of His children and that He would faithfully see them through every circumstance. While He knew life wouldn't always be pleasant, Jesus understood that God was in control and that He promised to work out every situation for the "good of those who love Him" (Romans 8:28).

Part of being our best for God involves learning to trust Him with the future. The Bible is full of stories that reaffirm His faithfulness. He delivers His people, defeats their enemies, saves them from trouble, and, ultimately, rescues them from sin and death through Jesus Christ. Knowing what He has done in the past and that He is the same faithful God today allows us to release our future into His hands, knowing He will pave a great path. While we won't always agree with His plan, we can trust that His way is better. But first we must believe what He says in His Word.

This is one reason it's so important for us to read the Bible daily. When we do, we are reminded of who God is—that He is the very definition of love and that He is always faithful. Then, when the voices of fear and anxiety raise questions in our minds about what lies ahead, we can return to the Truth we've read and remember that God is in control.

It's a simple concept that works for Charlotte Smith.

"I have to trust and believe that, even though my circumstances might suggest otherwise, God does have a perfect plan for my life," Smith said. "When I read Scripture and verses like Jeremiah 29:11, I am reminded that He has a future and a hope for me."

Releasing anxiety about the future is a challenge, but it's a challenge for everyone. And the good news is that the Word of God is for everyone, too. If you place your faith in Him, the Bible assures you that He will never leave you, that your path is secure, that He's in control, and that He has a plan. Once you truly believe that, you'll be able to embrace His peace and walk confidently forward into the days ahead.

Your Turn

What is your biggest fear about the future? _____

_____

_____

_____

When do you battle this fear the most? _____

_____

_____

_____

Why do you think Jesus told us so many times not to be afraid?

_____

_____

_____

_____

What are five verses you can memorize that will help you trust

God with your future? _____

_____

_____

_____

Being Your Best for God:
Look forward to the future!

"But what about you?" he asked. "Who do you say I am?" Simon Peter answered, "You are the Messiah, the Son of the living God." —Matthew 16:15-16

NAME: Kyle Korver

TEAM: Chicago Bulls

POSITION: Guard/Forward

HIGHLIGHTS: NBA record holder for three-point field goal percentage in a season (2009–10)

Great things can be passed down through genetics. Height, intelligence, appearance, skills—it's amazing what God can do with a little DNA.

In the case of NBA guard Kyle Korver, an aptitude for the game of basketball was one feature woven into his body's chemistry. Korver cultivated his God-given talent through hard work, good coaching, and healthy competition from his basketball-playing brothers, and eventually made it to the NBA, becoming well-known for his deadly three-point jump shot.

Genetics can transfer many fine qualities from parents to children. But there are certain things that just can't be passed down through the flesh. One of them is faith.

The oldest of four boys and the son of a pastor, Korver doesn't recall a time when he wasn't a Christian. It was part of his family's lifestyle, and it was all he'd ever known. His parents raised him with an understanding of God's Word and the knowledge that Jesus Christ was his Savior. Still, that information remained more in Korver's head than in his heart until he was drafted out of Creighton University into the high-profile world of the NBA.

In his new position under the spotlight of professional sports, Korver found himself confronting challenges he'd not faced in the Midwest. Removed from the comforts of home and the influence of his Christian family, Korver realized how much he'd relied on their faith to facilitate his own. He began to question if he really believed what he'd been taught. And, if he did, why was he feeling so empty and alone?

"I found myself saying, 'God, I want more than this. There is more than this, and I know that. Show me,'" Korver said.

Soon the young basketball star realized he'd been surviving on environmental faith instead of surrendering to Christ as the Lord of his life.

"I'd fallen into the trap of living to be a good person, not living for God," Korver said. "So I just poured my heart out to God and said, 'I don't want this anymore. I want You to change my heart.'"

Just like Korver, there comes a time for all of us when we must choose whether or not to truly follow Christ and engage in a personal relationship with Him. This kind of faith can't be passed on through our family, our friends, our culture, or our history; it has to be our choice—a conscious transfer of our life's ownership to the Lord. We must proclaim that we personally believe Jesus Christ is the Son of God, who conquered sin and death on our behalf, and then begin living in relationship with Him as our Lord.

> **"I'd fallen into the trap of living to be a good person, not living for God."**

Take a look at Matthew 16:13-17 and the account of the apostle Peter:

> When Jesus came to the region of Caesarea Philippi, he asked his disciples, "Who do people say the Son of Man is?"
>
> They replied, "Some say John the Baptist; others say Elijah; and still others, Jeremiah or one of the prophets."
>
> "But what about you?" he asked. "Who do you say I am?"

> Simon Peter answered, "You are the Christ, the Son of the living God."
>
> Jesus replied, "Blessed are you, Simon son of Jonah, for this was not revealed to you by man, but by my Father in heaven."

Imagine yourself in this situation. If you were walking with Jesus and you'd heard the varying opinions of others regarding His identity, how would you have responded to His question? Would you have been as bold as Peter, who gave a clear opinion, or would you have been vague and noncommittal, reasoning with Jesus by reciting answers you'd heard from others?

When we base our faith on what we've heard from others, we avoid the responsibility of making a decision for ourselves—an action revealing that we are either too scared to believe one way or too lazy to investigate Jesus Christ and His claims for ourselves. While putting off a decision about Christ might be an easy option, do we really want to leave the decision about our eternity up for grabs? If not, then we must make a decision about our personal faith.

Kyle Korver was brave enough to choose. Once he realized he'd been living on the faith of his family, he decided that wasn't good enough. He made up his mind to pursue a personal relationship with Christ. The result for Korver was deep fulfillment outside of anything the NBA had to offer.

If you, like Korver, want to be your best for God, start by establishing a foundation of personal faith in and surrender to Jesus Christ. Ask yourself if you are truly living a faith of your own or relying on others to determine what you believe. The choice is yours, and it's an important one. Don't leave it undecided.

Your Turn

Who or what outside influences affect what you believe about Christ? _____

_____

_____

_____

Do you believe that Jesus is the Son of God and that He died for your sins and was resurrected? If so, do you live by His Word, and have you made Him the Lord of your life? _____

_____

_____

_____

If not, what are you waiting for? _____

_____

_____

_____

Being Your Best for God:
Make your faith *your* faith.

dreams
come true

*Take delight in the Lord, and he will give you
the desires of your heart.* —Psalm 37:4

NAME: Sara Hall

SPORT: Professional Runner

HIGHLIGHTS: 2006 CVS Pharmacy Downtown 5K champion
Seven-time NCAA All-American (Stanford University)

ometimes you just know. That was the case for professional runner Sara Hall when, as a child, she first heard about international missions. She just knew that was what she was born to do. It was just a matter of letting God bring it all together.

After discovering her athletic gifts, Hall signed on to compete in cross country at Stanford University. While there, she not only starred on the team as a seven-time All-American but also met her future husband, fellow runner Ryan Hall. After graduating, the two were married and began their careers as professional runners. For Sara, though, the inner desire to reach the world for Christ remained alive in her heart.

Thankfully, the desire to reach the nations was shared by her husband, and soon, through the Halls' marital teamwork, they were able to utilize their distance-running platforms to reach the world. Partnering with the organization World Vision, the couple raised funds and awareness for clean water projects in Africa and even traveled there to help with the relief effort. It wasn't long before they established their own organization, the Hall Steps Foundation, in order to combat world poverty.

For Sara Hall, it was the fulfillment of a long-held desire.

"Through my faith and dedication to the Lord, He not only gave me exceptional experiences through running, He also fulfilled my childhood dream of mission work," Hall said. "God created me to be a world-changer and to help others in need, and I've been blessed to be able to do just that."

Just like Hall, we all have been given certain desires by God. Sometimes, however, He establishes them inside us before revealing how He will satisfy them. In fact, that's very often the case as part of the journey of faith we get to experience. He does this, in part, so that we will continually seek Him and pursue a relationship with Him. By giving us desires that only He can fulfill, He creates an open line of communication with us as we come to Him in the longing to see those dreams realized.

> "God created me to be a world-changer and to help others in need, and I've been blessed to be able to do just that."

Hall knew she was born to change the world, but instead of just signing up for a long-term mission project and getting on a plane, she followed the Lord's unique plan. By trusting in and waiting on Him, she was able to receive two major gifts she'd need for her journey: a platform and a partner. Through her gift of running, Hall found both her husband and fame in the endurance community, which helped her generate awareness for the cause so close to her heart.

"I never wanted an ordinary life, but to be extraordinary for God's kingdom," Hall said. "And because He is faithful, I know I will see His promises fulfilled."

Psalm 37:4 is an often-quoted verse that addresses inner longings. It says, "Take delight in the Lord, and he will give you the desires of your heart." While many think this is a blank check from God offering to give us everything we want, it actually goes much deeper.

According to this verse, when we are living for the Lord (taking "delight" in Him), He will place certain desires in our hearts that He wants to fulfill in His unique way. It may not be our anticipated or chosen path, but if we seek and follow Him, He promises to satisfy those longings. These desires can be any number of things from missions work to sports, jobs, spouses, or even the salvation of loved ones. The point is simply that God-given desires will have God-given results.

Being your best for God involves surrendering your personal desires to Him and trusting that He will fulfill them in His time and according to His plan. Sara Hall handed her desire for overseas missions to the Lord and focused on using her running gifts to bring Him glory. In the end, He used those very talents to fulfill her childhood dream in a way she never expected. If you're willing to trust Him with your longings and your life, you can know He'll do the same for you.

Your Turn

What is the deepest desire of your heart? _____

_____

_____

_____

Have you asked the Lord if it is a desire He has given you? How can you know? _____

_____

_____

Have you surrendered that desire to the Lord? Do you trust Him to fulfill it in His way? _____

_____

_____

Do you trust that His way is best? What if it is different from your plans? _____

_____

_____

Being Your Best for God:
Fulfillment comes from following God's plan.

being your best for God//

perseverance

> >   >   >   > >   >   >

 Perseverance: continued effort to do or achieve something despite difficulties, failure, or opposition

Therefore, since we are surrounded by such a great cloud of witnesses, let us throw off everything that hinders and the sin that so easily entangles, and let us run with perseverance the race marked out for us.
—Hebrews 12:1

a sure
foundation

*Jesus Christ is the same yesterday and
today and forever.* —Hebrews 13:8

NAME: Josh Hamilton

TEAM: Texas Rangers

POSITION: Outfielder

HIGHLIGHTS: 2010 AL MVP
2010 AL Batting Champion
MLB All-Star (2008–2010)

Josh Hamilton was only eighteen when he was suddenly stripped of the two things he had relied on most: his parents and baseball.

After being drafted out of his North Carolina high school by the Tampa Bay Rays, Hamilton was just starting spring training as a rookie when he and his parents were in a devastating car accident.

While Hamilton's parents—who had moved with their son to the training site in Florida—survived, they were forced to return to North Carolina for rehab. And as for the young ballplayer himself, Hamilton was forced to take time off the field in order to recover from his injuries.

For a teenager on his own for the first time, the drastic change in situation—the loss of everything familiar—meant one thing: trouble.

"That was the beginning of my downward spiral," Hamilton said.

His life now completely unrecognizable, Hamilton turned to outside sources to cope with the changes. First came tattoos, which still cover his body, and then came drugs. Within months, Hamilton was a full-blown addict.

Even after he'd recovered from the accident and returned to the field, drugs continued to cause chaos in his life. Before his career could take off, Hamilton found himself in repeated violation of the MLB drug policy and officially suspended from the game.

"I remember being at the field the next day and starting to cry because I knew what I had done," said Hamilton, citing the final game before his suspension. "I looked at the pitcher and realized that it might be the last time I ever stepped foot on the field."

Life is full of surprises, isn't it? We've all been blind-sided by moments that have permanently redirected our courses. Car accidents, natural disasters, job losses, deaths—all have the ability to alter our lives beyond recognition and shove us unwittingly into the unfamiliar. And, when those times come as they certainly will, if we lack a solid personal foundation we'll wind up grasping for stability in all the wrong places.

> "I'm so happy that God gives you more than one chance.... God's mercy and grace are astonishing to me."

When Josh Hamilton was thrown into a new lifestyle, he quickly realized that his identity wasn't rooted in anything permanent. He'd placed his security in people and sports, and, when both were taken away, he was forced to find ways to replace the stability they had seemed to provide. Thus, he turned to addiction. The tattoos and drugs became his new normal. And the same thing can happen to any of us during times of change if we derive our identity from earthly sources.

Part of being our best for God means being grounded in our identity as His children above all else. That means we don't draw personal worth from roles as athletes, coaches, students, sons, daughters, computer programmers, writers, etc. We are, above all, God's beloved children. And when firmly rooted in that truth, we will be able to endure life-altering situations without being forced to find a new identity. We'll be the same children of God that we were before, just in new circumstances. It's the only stable source of identity available.

According to James 1:17, God "does not change like shifting shadows"—and what is life more like than one big shifting shadow? Everything is conditional and circumstantial. The only thing that will never be altered is Jesus Christ and His love for us. He alone will remain constant through all situations. As Hebrews 13:8 says, "Jesus Christ is the same yesterday and today and forever."

When it comes to our ever-changing world, it's important to know that the unchanging Christ has offered to be our rock and salvation and to provide us with the stability that we crave. Josh Hamilton made this discovery for himself, and he now lives and competes as a child of God, bringing glory to His heavenly Father who saved him from certain destruction.

"I'm so happy that God gives you more than one chance," said Hamilton, who recovered from addiction and became an All-Star outfielder for the Texas Rangers. "When I decided to surrender my life to Christ, that was when it changed. God's mercy and grace are astonishing to me."

Today, if you are clinging to anything other than Christ for security and identity, think about what it would be like to lose it. If that thought brings anxiety or fear, surrender it to the Lord and ask Him to retake the top spot in your heart and ground you in this unchanging love. Then, enjoy His stability and let Him build you a sure foundation.

Your Turn

Where do you find your identity? _____

_____

_____

_____

What are some things you would find it difficult to lose?

_____

_____

_____

What does it mean to be a child of God? _____

_____

_____

_____

Is your identity found in being His child? If not, how would your

life be different if it were? _____

_____

_____

Being Your Best for God:
Endure change with an unchangeable Lord.

comeback kid

I have told you these things, so that in me you may
have peace. In this world you will have trouble. But
take heart! I have overcome the world. —John 16:33

NAME: Chris Klein

TEAMS: Kansas City Wizards (Sporting KC)
Real Salt Lake
LA Galaxy

POSITION: Midfielder

HIGHLIGHTS: Two-time MLS Comeback Player of the Year
MLS record holder for most consecutive games
played and consecutive games started

Most great sports stories involve a good comeback. Chris Klein's involves two.

In 2000, as a rising MLS star, Klein helped guide the Kansas City Wizards to an MLS Cup Championship revealing himself as one of the brightest talents in the game. But just a year later, after helping the Wizards make another postseason run, Klein tore the ACL in his right knee and was forced to battle back through physical rehab.

As a man of faith, though, Klein knew he wasn't in the process alone. He maintained his faith and believed the promises of God, trusting that He would reveal a divine purpose for the trial.

"I knew that no matter what happened, God was going to use it for good," Klein said of the injury. "I didn't know how it was going to look, but I knew it was going to happen."

In a remarkably quick recovery, Klein returned in 2002 and earned the league's Comeback Player of the Year Award after tallying seven goals and five assists in just twenty-five games. But in 2004, after being named an All-Star for the second time, Klein's patience and faith were once again tested by injury. This time it was a torn ACL in his left knee.

During his second injury, though, an amazing thing happened. Whereas many athletes would have become angry and frustrated with God for allowing such a thing to happen twice, Klein actually felt *greater* peace. Because he'd been through the situation before, he knew the Lord could do great things through the injury rehabilitation process. Klein simply applied what he'd learned the first go-round, and, through the Lord's strength, once again returned to his game in top form, being named the league's Comeback Player of the Year for the second time.

"Without Christ through both injuries I would have felt helpless and panicked," he said. "But with Him I felt confident. I knew that I was going to be okay."

In sports and in life we're all going to get hurt. It's almost a rite of passage, and we love to share the stories behind old battle scars. More often than not, though, it's not the injuries themselves that make those stories so special; it's what we learned through them.

As humans, we tend to view pain and suffering negatively, but because He sees a bigger picture, God views them differently. He knows that the recovery process can draw out positive things He's placed inside (like strength, patience, and endurance) which can only be developed through adversity. If we, like Chris Klein, learn to embrace setbacks as divine opportunities and focus on cultivating our faith through the recovery, we will be able to endure them with peace and joy.

> **"Without Christ through both injuries I would have felt helpless and panicked."**

In John 16:33, Jesus said, "I have told you these things, so that in me you may have peace. In this world you will have trouble. But take heart! I have overcome the world."

Having peace and confidence during injuries—or any setback, for that matter—isn't foolish or arrogant; it's biblical. The world often tells us that we have to be angry or frustrated as we endure trials, but that's not what Christ tells us. By relying on Him and trusting His promises, we can, through His strength, work our way back without losing our cool.

Today, if you are experiencing a difficult challenge like recovering from an injury, remind yourself that God has a positive take on the situation. He sees the good things He has planned for you, and He can't wait for you to discover them for yourself. Trust Him and follow His leading. Receive the strength He gives you through His Holy Spirit and persevere with joy knowing that you're receiving a great comeback story of your own.

Your Turn

Have you ever experienced a serious injury? If so, what was your attitude through it? _____

_____

_____

_____

How have setbacks made you stronger physically, mentally, and

spiritually? _____

_____

_____

_____

What kind of attitude would you expect from an injured Christ-

follower? _____

_____

_____

_____

How can our faith amid trials be a witness for Christ?

_____

_____

_____

_____

Being Your Best for God:
Let God give you a divine comeback story.

Before I formed you in the womb I knew you, before you were born I set you apart. —Jeremiah 1:5

NAME: DeLisha Milton-Jones

TEAM: Los Angeles Sparks

POSITION: Forward

HIGHLIGHTS: Two-time WNBA Champion
Two-time Olympic gold medalist
WNBA All-Star

WNBA All-Star DeLisha Milton-Jones is physically beautiful. One look at her team photo will tell you that. So it may come as a surprise to learn that she has ever been self-conscious about her appearance. But that's what happens when you have an eighty-four inch wingspan setting you apart from other women.

From fingertip to fingertip, Milton-Jones' arm length is the equivalent of a seven-foot man. While it may help her on the basketball court, it's not something most people see every day or would consider "normal." But it's the body God gave her, and Milton-Jones has learned to both embrace it and maximize it for His glory.

"On the court, I'm going to use every inch I can to my advantage," said Milton-Jones, a Christian since age eleven. "When girls get comfortable and put the ball in front of me, they forget that my wingspan is so long. Before they know it, I've gotten the ball out of their hands and we're going the other way."

Athletes often look different than their peers. They may be taller, more muscular, or, in the case of some, not muscular enough. And being different can be uncomfortable. Because we all have a natural desire to fit in, anything that sets us apart can seem, in our minds, like physical flaws.

But Milton-Jones has learned that this isn't the case.

"It's okay to be different," she says. "Sometimes being different is not going to be the most popular thing, but you have to be confident and know that, at the end of the day, you're covered by the Lord."

The issue of body image is often associated with women. They're told that the thin-yet-curvy magazine cover models are the picture of beauty, and that anything not matching that is not acceptable.

But it's not just girls. Guys feel it too. That ultra-lean frame they were born with may help them in cross country, but it doesn't resemble the guy on the cover of muscle magazines. Does that mean they should stop running and start drinking protein shakes? Not according to God's Word.

> **"It's okay to be different.... Be confident and know that, at the end of the day, you're covered by the Lord."**

In Psalm 139:13–14, David's words provide reassurance: "For you created my inmost being; you knit me together in my mother's womb. I praise you because I am fearfully and wonderfully made; your works are wonderful, I know that full well."

According to Scripture, we are amazing creations knit together specifically by the hand of God. All of our physical features were designed by Him and created to bring Him glory. God doesn't want us to think of our large hands or long legs as curses. Instead, He wants us to realize that He gave them to us as gifts—unique characteristics to both bring Him glory and help us in our calling.

No two people were created exactly the same. We are each a unique, divine child of God, and no one else can do exactly what we can. There isn't one other person who can live out our divine calling; it's ours alone to embrace and experience, and physical stature is a key part of that plan. Whether or not we simply learn to live with our perceived physical "curses" or hold them against God is our choice. We can either be angry at Him for how He created us, or we can embrace His truth, which says that we are beautiful or handsome just as God made us. And that source is far more credible than the ever-changing opinion of the world.

Beauty is in the eye of the beholder, and the ultimate Beholder says that we are perfectly crafted in His image. Short, tall, thick, thin, gangly, bald—whatever! If God made us in a specific way, then that is our picture of perfection—and the world can't argue otherwise. The sooner we embrace our physical quirks as blessings, the sooner we will be freed up to use them to bring glory to our Father.

DeLisha Milton-Jones is a great example. Once she embraced her arm length, she put it to good use by earning two Olympic gold medals and two WNBA titles. Follow her lead and be your best for God by looking in the mirror and recognizing the God-designed creation staring back at you. Then take joy in the reflection knowing that you were created for a purpose just as you are.

Your Turn

Have you ever wished you could change something about your appearance? What was it? _____

_____

_____

What do you think or feel about yourself when you look at a

magazine cover model? _____

_____

_____

Have you considered the ways that your unique physical

characteristics can be used to bring glory to God? _____

_____

_____

_____

What does Psalm 139 say about who you are in God's eyes? ____

_____

_____

_____

Being Your Best for God:
Love the look God gave you!

trial to triumph

They will have no fear of bad news; their hearts are steadfast, trusting in the Lord. —Psalm 112:7

NAME: Bethany Hamilton

SPORT: Professional Surfing

HIGHLIGHTS: 2004 ESPY Comeback Athlete of the Year
Second Place, 2009 Billabong ASP World Junior
Championship

Pro surfer Bethany Hamilton didn't plan on setting an example of faith through tragedy. She never woke up thinking that it would be the day she'd be attacked by a shark and nearly lose her life. She never imagine that this would be the answer to her prayers of becoming a role model of perseverance and courage. But as it stands today, that's exactly what she's become.

As a promising thirteen-year-old amateur surfer, Hamilton made national news on October 31, 2003, when she was attacked by a fourteen-foot tiger shark and lost her left arm. National media captured the story, and soon Hamilton was put on display in front of a global audience. As a follower of Christ, the young surfer maintained a positive attitude and soon captivated the world with her stance of faith. Viewers were shocked by how peaceful Hamilton remained through the tragedy, and they marveled even more when she returned to the water just weeks later to resume her up-and-coming career.

Having been raised in a Christian home, Hamilton had surrendered her life to the Lord before the attack. She knew that He had a purpose for all of life's situations. This truth was further solidified in her heart when she recalled a prayer she had said just weeks before the attack.

"In early October 2003, my mom and I started asking God to use me and to show me His purpose for my life," Hamilton said. "After the shark attack, I accepted that God allowed it to happen for a reason. Through it, I just want people to see that my hope and strength come from Jesus Christ."

Tragedies are hard to understand. In moments of pain, it can be almost impossible for us to see anything other than what we've lost. But if we have placed our faith in Christ, we can choose to believe that trials come to us so that God's greater glory can be revealed.

> **"I just want people to see that my hope and strength come from Jesus Christ."**

Bethany Hamilton wouldn't have chosen the road of pain, but when it unfolded before her, she embraced it as God's best plan. It wasn't easy, and there were moments of tears, but Hamilton's faith helped her rise above the situation and bring honor to her heavenly Father—the One who had known all along that she was capable of handling tragedy with grace.

Not everyone could have done what Hamilton did. It's rare to find someone who has a faith strong enough to endure extreme challenges with peace and trust. But in His intimate understanding of His children, God knows who is strong enough to bear witness of Him through trials.

FYI: You are one of them.

Odds are you've already lived through your share of hardship. They're just part of life. And the longer we live, the more challenges we experience. The question simply boils down to whether or not we are spiritually prepared to handle them when they happen. Will we trust the Lord enough to respond in faith and believe in His sovereign plan, or will we blame Him for allowing such devastation?

Jeremiah 29:11 is one of the most quoted verses in the Bible for good reason: because we all can relate. It says, "'For I know the plans I have for you,' declares the Lord, 'plans to prosper you and not to harm you, plans to give you hope and a future.'"

When unexpected challenges arise, no matter how big or small, it should comfort us to know that the Lord had a plan for it from the beginning. He had already woven it into His perfect design for our lives and created a way to work it out for our benefit (Romans 8:28).

Today, whatever you are facing, remember that the Lord has your best interest in mind. He loves you and wants to bless you if you will only trust Him. Choose to be your best for God by embracing His plan and allowing Him to reveal it to you. Cling to His Word and trust in His love. Then, just like Bethany Hamilton, watch as He turns your trial into triumph for His kingdom.

Your Turn

What is the most difficult thing you've ever experienced?

Can you see ways in which God used it to draw you closer to Him?

_____

_____

_____

What challenge are you currently facing and how are you responding? _____

_____

_____

_____

Do you trust that the Lord has a good plan even in trials? Why?

_____

_____

_____

Being Your Best for God:
Triumph over trials with trust.

remember
to
remember

God has said, "Never will I leave you; never will I forsake you." —Hebrews 13:5

NAME: Jeff Francoeur

TEAM: Kansas City Royals

POSITION: Right Fielder

HIGHLIGHTS: 2007 Gold Glove Award Winner

Every time there's a thunderstorm, MLB outfielder Jeff Francoeur is reminded of God's grace. It's not just that he feels largely humbled by the One who creates the weather, though that would be true. It's something much smaller—just a slight tingle in his face. Yet even small twinges can be big reminders.

For Francoeur, that tingle marks the spot where, on July 7, 2004, a 95-mph fastball smashed into his cheekbone as he was squaring around to bunt in what should have been his final at-bat for the Class-A Myrtle Beach Pelicans. Instead of making his way up the minor-league ladder as he'd intended, however, Francoeur found himself in a hospital bed just hoping he'd be able to see again. All the plans he'd made to become the starting right fielder for the Atlanta Braves by the start of the next season would have to be put on hold while doctors worked to repair his face.

Being a Christian, Francoeur did the only thing he knew to do. He trusted God and stayed focused on the Lord's plan at the surrender of his own. And in a matter of divine timing, Francoeur's big-league dream eventually came true when he took his place in the Braves' lineup and stepped onto his first major league field exactly one year after the accident.

To Francoeur, the incident, the timing, and even the metal plate inserted in his face all offered confirmation that God was in charge and that He had been from the beginning.

"Sometimes in this game you can get lost in doing things for yourself and just being selfish," Francoeur said. "But you have to remember that it's God who has allowed you to do what you do. He's put you in a great position to give glory to Him."

"Remember." It's a great word, isn't it? It allows us to go back in time and revisit the moments when God revealed Himself and proved Himself faithful. By reflecting on His past deliverances, we can recall how He stood by us and carried us through trial after trial. Almost instantly, our faith is strengthened by recalling that because He was with us before, He will be with us again.

> **"You have to remember that it's God who has allowed you to do what you do. He's put you in a great position to give glory to Him."**

Looking at Scripture, we find that remembering is more than just a good idea; it's something that God actually instructed us to do. Isaiah 46:9 says, "Remember the former things, those of long ago; I am God, and there is no other; I am God, and there is none like me." When we recall His works of the past, we are reminded of who He is and what He's done, which helps us trust Him with what's to come.

Remember the time the Lord helped you through the career-threatening injury? Remember the time He comforted you when you lost a loved one? Remember the time you thought you couldn't go on and He led you to just the right Scripture? Looking back, we can see His fingerprints on our lives. Even though our experiences might have been painful to endure, we were delivered through them by the one true God, who loves us. Even if the results weren't what we desired, He still had a divine plan and never left us to deal with them on our own.

The same God who gave Jeff Francoeur both a metal plate and a dream-come-true is the One who has walked every step of our past with us and continues to plot out our futures. But since not all of us are given lightning-triggered facial twinges as memory tools, we must be diligent to remember His faithfulness in other ways. One good way to do that is by journaling. When we record the acts of God, we can reflect on them when times get tough and remember how He carried us through.

Another powerful way to remember is by staying in fellowship with other believers. When brothers and sisters in Christ walk through our trials with us, they are able to remind us of His faithfulness after witnessing it for themselves.

Finally, spending time with the Lord through prayer and reading His Word helps us remember. When we communicate with Him, He reminds us of the powerful history we share and speaks His faithfulness into our souls.

Today, if you truly want to be your best for God, don't forget to remember. A good way to start this practice is by meditating on Hebrews 13:5, which reminds us that God will never leave His children. That truth alone will give you encouragement no matter what challenge comes your way. Even if it's a 95-mph fastball.

Your Turn

How does remembering the past victories help you in the present?

_____

_____

How does it help you prepare for the future? _____

_____

_____

Can you think of a time when remembering God's faithfulness in

past trials helped you through a situation later? _____

_____

_____

Do you practice remembering God's faithfulness? How? _____

_____

_____

Being your best for God:
Don't forget to remember.

wonderfully made

*I praise you because I am fearfully and
wonderfully made; your works are wonderful,
I know that full well.* —Psalm 139:14

NAME: Tamika Catchings

TEAM: Indiana Fever

POSITION: Forward

HIGHLIGHTS: Seven-time WNBA All-Star
WNBA All-Decade team
Four-time WNBA Defensive Player of the Year
(2005, 2006, 2009, 2010)
Two-time Olympic Gold Medalist

As the face of the Indiana Fever, WNBA All-Star Tamika Catchings has become a role model for athletes across the globe. Throughout her career, she's earned just about every award possible in the sport of women's basketball, including All-American nods at the University of Tennessee, ESPY awards, Olympic gold medals, and WNBA league honors.

But as a Christian, Catchings doesn't see her awards as avenues for personal glory. Instead, she uses them to honor the One who blessed her with ability and delivered her through difficult challenges.

"I live my life in a way that I know He would want, and I live as Christlike as I can from this platform," Catchings said. "God keeps me focused on where I'm going in life. He protects me. He provides for me. He guides me, and He leads me."

Watching her play with ease and grace on the court, it's hard to imagine that Catchings had anything but a streamlined road to success. But as a child, Catchings was a shy young woman born with a hearing disability that threatened to cripple her social skills. Kids can be cruel, and growing up, Catchings' classmates were ruthless in their comments regarding her condition. She grew to despise her hearing aids and her speech impediment, and she longed only to remain on the basketball court or in the classroom where she didn't have to talk.

Thankfully, the Lord had the final say. What human eyes viewed as negative, He worked out as a positive providing Catchings with an athletic ability that would help her deal with life.

"Sports helped me excel and get through that," Catchings said. "Over time, it was something that helped me develop my never-give-up attitude."

Through His Word, God reveals that He purposely and uniquely designs each of His children. Psalm 139:15–16 says, "My frame was not hidden from you when I was made in the secret place, when I was woven together in the depths of the earth. Your eyes saw my unformed body."

According to this psalm, God created Tamika Catchings just as she was—hearing disability and all. Just because she didn't speak or hear like her friends didn't mean she was weak or useless. In fact, though she may have lacked in one area, she very much excelled in another.

> "God keeps me focused on where I'm going in life. He protects me. He provides for me. He guides me, and He leads me."

What a perfect example of God's love and plan for us all. While we can't help but view circumstances as being either positive or negative, in reality, that is not our call to make. The world told Tamika Catchings that her hearing disability was a bad thing, but through that challenge she developed priceless character traits like her "never-give-up attitude."

In life, we tend to think that anything causing emotional or physical pain is bad and anything bringing immediate joy is good.

But God has a different evaluation system—one in which He knows the plan and the blessings He wants to give us through each trial. It is our choice, however, to believe His system or our own. We can either view each challenge as negative because it causes us pain, or trust the Lord to make it part of our beautiful testimony.

Tamika Catchings' hearing disability contributed to her great success on the basketball court. And, just like Catchings, we all face obstacles. Maybe they're physical; maybe they're emotional. Regardless of what they may be, God knows exactly what will happen and has made a plan to use it for our good. While that may be hard to see, it's the truth. He loves us and has a plan to restore even the most broken places of our hearts if we let Him.

Whatever you've been through or are going through now, choose to be your best for God by trusting Him with the situation and allowing Him to reveal His plan. You may have to wait days, weeks, or even years to see the blessings, but you can depend on the One who has a good purpose in mind.

Your Turn

*What has been the most difficult or painful situation you've experienced?*_____

_____

_____

_____

Looking back, what was one positive thing that came out

of that situation? _____

_____

_____

_____

How are you a stronger person for having endured emotional and

physical pain? _____

_____

_____

_____

How can your past trials be part of your faith story? _____

_____

_____

_____

_____

Being Your Best for God:
Let pain equal gain by trusting the Lord.

> > > > > > > > > > > > >

being your best for God//

action

Action: an act of will; a thing done

Therefore everyone who hears these words of mine and puts them into practice is like a wise man who built his house on the rock. —Matthew 7:24

strength
in numbers

*Two are better than one, because they have a good
return for their labor: if either of them falls down,
one can help the other up. But pity anyone who falls
and has no one to help them up.* —Ecclesiastes 4:9–10

NAME: Chris Kaman

TEAM: Los Angeles Clippers

POSITION: Center

HIGHLIGHTS: 2010 NBA All-Star

It may seem like a lifestyle choice made to suit LA, but it's actually just the opposite.

"Everybody calls it my 'entourage,' but it's really not," said NBA center Chris Kaman. "They're just some buddies who are good accountability partners. They help me keep my head above water and keep me from getting a big ego."

After graduating from the University of Central Michigan and being drafted by the Los Angeles Clippers in 2003, Kaman knew he needed to do whatever he could in order to maintain his walk with Christ—especially considering he was now a celebrity living in one of the most status-minded cities in the world. In order to combat the self-absorbed lifestyle, Kaman recruited three Christian friends to live with him in LA and be a spiritual support system. According to Kaman, the group helped him keep things "real" around the house and allowed him to stand up to the temptations of celebrity life.

"I don't ever want to be someone who thinks he's better than anyone else or thinks he needs special treatment, which can happen in this lifestyle," he said. "I want to be pleasant with everybody, and I want to be approachable. I think these guys help me stay accountable to that."

According to God's Word, Kaman made a wise move. Ecclesiastes 4:9-10 says, "Two are better than one, because they have a good return for their labor: if either of them falls down, one can help the other up. But pity anyone who falls and has no one to help them up."

Kaman understood that living above reproach in a tempting environment required help, and that, with the teamwork of Christian friends, he was better equipped to sidestep the common pitfalls of a career in the NBA.

The same concept applies to us all. If we truly desire to be our best for God, we need the help and accountability of others. We need people in our lives who can ask us the tough questions and help us keep it together when we are tempted to make ungodly choices.

> **"I don't ever want to be someone who thinks he's better than anyone else or thinks he needs special treatment."**

While most Christians acknowledge the importance of accountability, few are willing to actually follow through with it. Accountability requires humility, honesty, time, submission, and courage—things that don't always come naturally. It's easier to live the life we want without having to answer to anyone. We like to feel free of responsibility and consequences—free to do what we want when we want without having to maintain a set of standards. We're tempted to think that, if we're living a "good" life in public, we can do anything in secret as long as no one ever finds out.

In reality, though, even when no one else sees what we do behind closed doors, God does. And it is to Him alone that we are ultimately accountable regardless of what we "get away with" here on earth.

According to Hebrews 4:13, "Nothing in all creation is hidden from God's sight. Everything is uncovered and laid bare before the eyes of him to whom we must give account."

Even if no one sees us getting drunk at the bar on Saturday night or visiting inappropriate websites at 1:00 a.m., the Lord does, and His opinion of our actions is ultimately the only one that matters. Regardless of what we may think, no sin is consequence-free. Even if no one sees them, they still cause us harm by putting more distance between us and God.

When we consider the facts, accountability starts to make a lot of sense. Why, then, would we not want to make it a part of our lives?

Today, if you truly desire to be your best for God, consider how the body of believers can help you. Seek out trusted Christian friends and advisors to hold you accountable and help you stay on God's best path for your life. You might even call in a "spiritual entourage" of your own.

Your Turn

Why is it important to be accountable to others?

Do you have accountability relationships in your life? Why or why not? _____

_____

_____

_____

How could your relationship with Christ be enhanced through accountability? _____

_____

_____

_____

Being Your Best for God:
Recruit an entourage of accountability.

*In your hearts revere Christ as Lord. Always
be prepared to give an answer to everyone
who asks you to give the reason for the hope
that you have. But do this with gentleness
and respect.* —1 Peter 3:1

NAME: Jon Kitna

TEAM: Dallas Cowboys

POSITION: Quarterback

HIGHLIGHTS: 2003 NFL Comeback Player of the Year

It's a shame that athletes are often stereotyped as being no brains and all brawn. Clearly, anyone who believes that has never played sports. It takes great intelligence to understand the intricacies of any game and even more to play it well.

The best athletes are often those who combine both mind and muscle. They know the ins and outs of their sport and are able to carry out the physical skills required.

NFL quarterback Jon Kitna has the classic appearance of a pro athlete. He's six-foot-two, 230 pounds of solid muscle. If anyone could be stereotyped as "all brawn," it would be Kitna. But for every ounce of physical power inside this NFL veteran, there's an equal amount of mental strength—something he puts to work for more than just football.

"I've been taught 1 Peter 3:15," said Kitna, who surrendered his life to Christ in the early 1990s. "The most important thing is to set Christ apart as Lord of my life. If I do that, then I don't have to beat people over the head with it; they'll come to me and ask questions. Then, as the verse goes on to say, I must be prepared to give an answer for the hope that I have and to do that with gentleness and respect."

By quoting Scripture so easily, Jon Kitna offers proof that there's more to him than physical strength. He is capable of discussing and debating a number of spiritual topics with great skill and one of his favorite subjects is the Bible. He is not afraid to go toe-to-toe with anyone about the truth of God's Word and the reality of Jesus because he knows what is written. He's studied Scripture, and he's investigated its truth.

"You become bolder and grow stronger the more you read the Bible," Kitna said.

When it comes to our depth of spiritual wisdom, we are often the ones who put limits on our understanding. God gave us brains with the anticipation that we would use them to seek Him intellectually. He's willing to take us as deep as we'll let Him go, but we often find excuses not to take Him up on the offer by making statements like, "I wouldn't understand the Bible, so I'm just not going to read it."

"You become bolder and grow stronger the more you read the Bible."

In the book of Proverbs, however, the Lord asks us to wise up and grow in our understanding of Him. Reading through the chapters, we find that wisdom is supreme (4:7), of more worth than gold (16:16), and something that we should actively seek every day. If we do, our paths will be level (3:5–6), our courses straight (15:21), and our footing sure (3:26).

Going through life without wisdom is like trying to run a marathon in sandals—it's an injury waiting to happen. Every day we face obstacles and we must be ready to hurdle each one or we'll be tripped up. Spiritually speaking, this means that we need to be equipped with God's truth and a fundamental understanding of His Word. If we aren't, we will fall more easily into sin, which will break much more than just our ankles.

All of us have been given the capacity for spiritual wisdom, and when it comes to being our best for God, we need to embrace it. Our Bibles weren't meant to sit on shelves and collect dust. God gave them to us so that we could read His game plan for life and carry it out. As a loving Father, He knows and wants what is best for us. The only way to achieve that is by following His instruction. It's just up to us to open the book and start learning.

Think about it this way. No skilled athlete would take the field without being well-versed in the team's plays. In the same way, you can't rush into life without understanding your spiritual playbook—the Bible. If you do, you'll get steamrolled by the competition. Instead, like Jon Kitna, use your God-given brainpower to study up for the biggest game of all: the game of life.

Your Turn

Why do you think it takes intelligence to play sports? _____

_____

_____

_____

_____

In what ways have you studied to get better athletically? How could this concept help you learn to study spiritually? _____

_____

_____

_____

How often do you study the Bible? What excuses have you made for avoiding it? _____

_____

_____

_____

What do you need to do in order to gain spiritual wisdom? _____

_____

_____

_____

_____

Being Your Best for God:
Exercise your mind.

Be still and know that I am God
—Psalm 46:10

NAME: Kara Lawson

TEAM: Connecticut Sun

POSITION: Guard

HIGHLIGHTS: 2005 WNBA Champion
2007 WNBA All-Star
Olympic Gold Medalist

WNBA guard and ESPN broadcaster Kara Lawson loves being active. She enjoys a full, vibrant environment and admits that she doesn't do well with downtime. That naturally energetic personality might be one reason she's had so much success on the hardwood.

After an All-American career at the University of Tennessee, Lawson was selected fifth overall in the 2003 WNBA Draft and made an immediate impact on the league. In 2005 she helped the Sacramento Monarchs win the WNBA championship, and in 2007 she was individually honored as a league All-Star. Then in 2008, she realized yet another athletic dream when she helped Team USA win a gold medal at the summer Olympics in Beijing.

But even high-energy athletes like Lawson need moments of peace in order to be their best for God.

"Being still is important for Christians because it's part of who God is," Lawson said. "God is stillness; He is peace in a chaotic world."

According to Lawson, there's a noticeable difference in her demeanor and attitude when she takes time to connect with God through quiet moments rather than rushing through each day without acknowledging Him.

"When I'm embracing still moments with God, I feel closer to Him. I make better decisions, have less of a temper, and am more tolerant," Lawson said. "When I'm not connecting with Him, small things or certain people become irritating. And I think that's one of the key indicators as to whether or not it's been awhile since I've really taken time to focus on Him."

The game of basketball is full of motion and activity. It's a fun, fast-paced sport in which there's always something going on. But, for those who play, it can also be exhausting and overwhelming. That's why teams take time-outs. In those brief moments on the sidelines, they are able to rest, regroup, and refocus so that they can return to the court with fresh minds and bodies.

> **"When I'm embracing still moments with God, I feel closer to Him. I make better decisions, have less of a temper, and I'm more tolerant."**

In many ways, life is a lot like basketball. At any given moment, there's a flurry of activity going on around us, and we're usually being pulled in a thousand different directions. Our schedules are packed, our inboxes are full, and our text message alerts won't stop beeping. It's the nature of the world today, and if we want to survive, we have to learn to take spiritual pauses.

Jesus prioritized time alone with His Father, and Scripture tells us that He often withdrew from crowds in order to find quiet places to pray. Through those times, He found refreshment by entering into fellowship with God—His Source of ultimate love, peace, and strength. And, if we want to grow spiritually, we need to follow His lead.

The benefits of quiet moments alone with the Lord are impossible to count. Through fellowship with the Father, our screaming souls are quieted and our over-anxious minds are set at ease. In those moments we are reminded that we serve a loving God who is constantly available to us and at work on our behalf.

In our solitude with Him, our tears can flow freely as we pour out our hurts. It is a safe place to be real and honest without fear of condemnation. In God's presence we are able to climb into His "everlasting arms" (Deuteronomy 33:27) and let Him speak peace and truth into our anxiety, fear, and confusion.

While it's easy to see the good that can come from being still before God, many of us find it hard to carve out the time. Most often our excuses tend to be rooted in either pride, which tells us that we are too important to step away from our connective devices or life situations, or fear, which says we must hide our shortcomings from God.

In reality, His presence is not something to be feared or avoided, but desired. It is filled with love, not condemnation, and His desire is to remind us of His faithfulness, renew our strength, and offer us His forgiveness through Christ. But this can only happen when we stop long enough to engage with Him.

In today's wired and chaotic world, being your best for God will involve prioritizing time alone with Him. When you carve out moments of stillness, you will find, just as Kara Lawson did, that life's circumstances are easier to handle. You'll realize that God loves you, that He's on your side, and that He is constantly available, willing to listen and eager to offer refreshment for your soul.

Your Turn

Do you spend time alone with God daily? Why or why not? _____

_____

_____

_____

What difference does it make in your attitude and lifestyle when

you are disconnected from God? _____

_____

_____

How would your life be better if you spent more time alone

with God? _____

_____

_____

How can you rework your schedule to prioritize these times? _____

_____

_____

Being Your Best for God:
Take a spiritual time-out.

washed by
the word

For the word of God is living and active. Sharper than any double-edged sword, it penetrates even to dividing soul and spirit, joints and marrow; it judges the thoughts and attitudes of the heart. —Hebrews 4:12

NAME: Luke Ridnour

TEAM: Minnesota Timberwolves

POSITION: Guard

HIGHLIGHTS: 2003 Pac-10 Player of the Year (University of Oregon)

On the outside, NBA guard Luke Ridnour looked like a typical, clean-cut athlete when he arrived on the campus of the University of Oregon in 2000. As a freshman, Ridnour was focused on developing his basketball skills in preparation for what he hoped would be a long career on the hardwood. Soon, though, he realized that the pressure to perform at such a high level was more than he could handle on his own.

"I'd put so much into the game of basketball that it was my idol," Ridnour said. "If I played well, I was up. If I played poorly, I was down. Everything depended on how I was on the court. I didn't have a way out. I never had peace."

That's when things began to change. Having been raised in a Christian home, Ridnour had accepted Christ as his Savior as a child. So when he began to search for something that would give him the inner peace basketball wouldn't, it didn't take long for him to find what he was looking for—maybe because, deep down, he'd known where to find it all along.

"When I started reading the Bible, everything changed," Ridnour said. "It impacted the way I thought, the way I acted, and my attitude. It started to change who I was. It was like being washed by the Word."

Ridnour's transformation wasn't the result of any effort he made on his own other than what it took to open his Bible. It was the work of the Holy Spirit who began speaking to him through the Scriptures. Through Ridnour's study of God's Word, he learned the truth about his identity as a child of God and his purpose as a follower of Christ. Soon he was living with peace and joy that had nothing to do with what happened on the court.

> "When I started reading the Bible, everything changed. It impacted the way I thought, the way I acted, and my attitude."

Hebrews 4:12 tells us just how powerful Scripture really is. According to this verse, the Bible is more than just a normal book; it's alive, active, and sharp. It has the power to cut into the deepest places of our hearts like no text ever written. Through it we are encouraged by hope, convicted of sin, comforted by love, and inspired by its divine Author.

Because so many evidential facts support the validity of the Bible, many of us don't have a problem believing its truth. Our greater difficulty often lies in picking it up and taking the time to read it at all. But an important question we need to ask ourselves is whether or not our lack of study is based on busyness—which can be corrected by altering our schedules—or if it is a deeper issue.

While many of us believe the basic truth that Jesus is the Son of God, and that, through Him, we receive forgiveness, redemption, and salvation, that's where we often want it to end. We'd rather stop at belief than actually go through the process of learning how to live for Him according to His plan. If we aren't willing to make lifestyle changes, we avoid reading the Bible altogether.

What would happen, though, if we faced our fear of change and opened God's Word to find out how He wants us to live? If we did, we'd find that God's ways are actually better than our own and that transformation at His hand is actually a good thing—not something to be feared but something to be desired based on its ability to bring deep, true fulfillment to our souls.

Luke Ridnour chose to open God's Word, and, as a result, experienced the kind of peace-giving, life-offering transformation that only takes place when we let God shape our lives. And the same thing can happen for us. By opening our Bibles and refusing to let the fear of conviction hold us back, we can embrace the same peace and joy available to us through Jesus Christ.

Today, if you want to be your best for God, start digging into Scripture on a regular basis and opening yourself up to its transforming power. Like Ridnour, be washed by the Word and enjoy the peace from the cleansing that it brings.

Your Turn

How often do you read the Bible? _____

_____

_____

_____

Was there a time when you read a verse and it changed you for the better? Explain. _____

_____

_____

_____

_____

Are you afraid of being convicted of your sin? If so, why? _____

_____

_____

_____

What are some ways you can begin to fill your mind with more of God's Word? _____

_____

_____

Being Your Best for God:
Find true transformation by reading His Word.

sharing the
spotlight

*In the same way, let your light shine before others,
that they may see your good deeds and glorify your
Father in heaven.* —Matthew 5:16

NAME: Matt Capps

TEAM: Minnesota Twins

POSITION: Pitcher

HIGHLIGHTS: 2010 MLB All-Star

Before every inning he pitches, Matt Capps takes a public stance of faith. He walks to the back of the pitchers' mound, removes his cap, and bows his head in prayer. He does this for two reasons. First, to ask the Lord for help in bringing Him glory. And second, to pray that someone watching from the stands would see this prayer and begin asking questions about faith.

Capps knows he's in the spotlight. He knows that thousands of eyes are on him when he's in the middle of the field, and he's not about to let the opportunity go by without pointing those eyes to Christ.

"If just one kid looks at his dad or mom when I'm praying and says, 'What's going on out there?' and they can explain it to him, then I've served my role in being out there," Capps said. "Being professional athletes, we are given certain gifts and talents, and there's a reason why. If God has blessed me with the ability to throw a baseball and I can share my faith and love for Him just by being out there and saying a prayer, then that's what I want to do."

Capps provides a great example of how to maximize an athletic platform. Every time he prays on the field, he reminds those watching that he is competing for Someone other than himself. And, through the stories he's heard in response—many from parents— Capps knows his public profession of faith is making a difference.

Part of being our best for God involves understanding and embracing our public platform. Even if we're not pro athletes, we're inevitably given a spotlight through either sports or our careers in general. Whether it's through the small crowd at a junior high volleyball game, a stadium full of Division-I college football fans, or coworkers in an office presentation, we often find ourselves in front of an audience. And what are they seeing? Of course they're noticing our skills, but they're also observing our actions, reactions, words, and outbursts. They notice if we react childishly to criticism, and they can certainly read our lips if we mutter under our breath. Thankfully, though, they also see the times when we respond out of patience, love, and hard work, and when, like Capps, we display our faith in Christ in a physical way.

> **"Being professional athletes, we are given certain gifts and talents, and there's a reason why. If God has blessed me with the ability to throw a baseball and I can share my faith and love for Him just by being out there and saying a prayer, then that's what I want to do."**

As Christians it's important for us to keep in mind just how much of a microscope we are under. Even if we're not the star of the team or don't have a big platform, we're still in front of a crowd, and how we conduct ourselves will either draw people closer to or further away from Christ. Something as simple as hustling back on defense in basketball, for example, reveals important elements of our character—that we work hard and value our team. Giving a half-hearted jog and making our teammates pick up the slack, however, reveals inner pride and disrespect. Both of these actions communicate a specific message, but only one reveals the character of Christ. And if we have identified ourselves as believers in Him, we are accountable to convey an accurate message.

In 1 John 3:18 we are told to communicate our love through actions and truth. Today, consider your place in the public eye and how you might communicate the love of Christ and the truth about Him to those who are watching. The eyes are on you. Follow the example of guys like Matt Capps and point them to the Lord.

Your Turn

Has anyone ever approached you and referenced a specific action or an emotion you displayed while in the spotlight? What did that say about your witness for Christ?

_____

_____

_____

_____

When you observe the emotions of athletes on TV, what do their expressions and words reveal about their character? _____

_____

_____

How can you tell the truth about Christ while in front of your specific audience? _____

_____

_____

What are some creative ways you can point the eyes of that audience to Christ? _____

_____

_____

_____

Being Your Best for God:
When eyes are on you, point them to Christ.

beyond belief

*People look at the outward appearance,
but the Lord looks at the heart.* —1 Samuel 16:7

NAME: Leah O'Brien Amico

SPORT: Softball

POSITION: Outfield

HIGHLIGHTS: Three-time Olympic gold medalist

There are many ways to define a "cultural Christian," but softball legend Leah O'Brien Amico doesn't need a dictionary. She knows exactly what it means based on firsthand experience.

"It was one of those things where I'd said a prayer, but my life didn't really change," said the three-time Olympic gold medalist. "I prayed, and I did believe in what Jesus promised, but I didn't have the truth of the Bible. I had more of a typical 'American Christianity'—just be a good person."

Growing up in California, Amico had appeared to be a great kid. She had good morals, was raised in a loving household, got excellent grades, and developed into an outstanding five-tool player on the softball field. But something happened to her between high school and her historic career with Team USA that redefined her life.

Signing on to play at the University of Arizona, Amico found herself under the influence of a Christian teammate—a young woman who set an example of genuine, Christlike love. Through their friendship, Amico realized she'd been living a virtual lie by professing a faith that she didn't truly understand. Yes, she believed intellectually that Jesus was the Son of God, but this belief hadn't made a difference in her lifestyle. She had a Bible, but because she didn't know what it said, she couldn't live out its principles.

Eventually, through the encouragement of her teammate, Amico began to desire and cultivate a personal relationship with

Christ and learn what it means to daily live for Him. The change resulted in a total life-transformation—one in which others could clearly see the person of Jesus modeled through her.

"God has created us for a bigger purpose," she said. "When we let Him lead, it's always better than we imagine."

It's not often that we have to strain to tell the difference between authentic and inauthentic Christians. There are clear distinctions in their lifestyle choices. While many who claim to be Christian will say they believe in Jesus, true people of faith actually embody Him by loving and serving others. More than just believing, they actually "walk" through each day with Christ and allow His love and joy to flow out of them into the world.

> "God has created us for a bigger purpose.... When we let Him lead, it's always better than we imagine."

For people who live in environments free of religious persecution, claiming Christianity even while living a contradictory lifestyle is easy. In the United States there are churches in every city and Bibles in almost every house. We're practically born into thinking we're Christian by default. But a mere religious title doesn't matter unless its subject has penetrated our souls.

According to 1 Samuel 16:7, "People look at the outward appearance, but the Lord looks at the heart." God knows the difference between those of us who are surrendered to Him and those of us who are offering up faith lip service. He knows every time we point to the sky after a goal on the field and then go out and get drunk with our friends. He's not fooled by superficial thanks when we succeed, nor is He flattered. He wants so much more than for us to be stuck in the miserable gray area between sin and sainthood. He wants our hearts to be fully and authentically His.

God has abundant blessings for each of us, but we must do more than just believe in order to discover them. In fact, mere belief itself will do nothing more than confirm what even the armies of darkness know. As James 2:19 says, "You believe that there is one God. Good! Even the demons believe that—and shudder." When we only believe in God intellectually without inviting Him into our lives, we sit on a level playing field with demons. They know God exists, too, but, just like we do when we stop at belief, they choose not to operate according to the Lord's standards.

When it comes to being our best for God, we must do more than just claim to be Christians; we must surrender our lives to Him completely and pursue a relationship with Him. If we seek His truth found in Scripture and live according to His ways, we will be transformed into obvious believers, set apart from the world. We will stand out as sources of His holy light and naturally draw others to Him.

Take it from Leah O'Brien Amico—once a cultural Christian who encountered authentic faith and was transformed as a result. Truly following the Lord is a real, personal venture that extends beyond words. Once you start to live it, neither your life nor those of the ones around you will ever be the same.

Your Turn

If you say you are a softball player but never step on a field or pick up a glove, are you really what you say you are? How does this concept apply to your spiritual life? _____

_____

_____

What is the difference between believing in Christ and living fully for Him? _____

_____

_____

Do you live out your faith, or are you stuck at belief? _____

_____

_____

What steps can you take to live out your faith more fully? _____

_____

_____

_____

Being Your Best for God:
Live what you say you believe.

being your best for God//

leadership

> >   >   >   > >   >   >

 Leadership: capacity to lead; to guide someone or something along a way

Follow my example, as I follow the example of Christ. —1 Corinthians 11:1

countering
the critics

Blessed are those who are persecuted because of righteousness,
for theirs is the kingdom of heaven. —Matthew 5:10

NAME: Mark Richt

TEAM: University of Georgia

POSITION: Head Football Coach

HIGHLIGHTS: Two-time SEC Coach of the Year (2002, 2005)

During his tenure at the University of Georgia, head football coach Mark Richt has had to take the bad with the good. No matter how tough things have been, however, he wouldn't trade any of it for a second. He loves his job and the responsibility that comes with it.

"When I first started coaching, I was drawn to it because of the strategy and competition," Richt said. "But the more I've coached, the more I've realized how great a responsibility we have for the young men God has put us in authority over. I take that part very seriously. I want to help these guys grow into good, godly men."

Richt first arrived at Georgia in 2001 and made an immediate positive impact on the program. He led the Bulldogs to Southeastern Conference Championships in 2002 and 2005, and was named SEC Coach of the Year in each of those seasons.

With his success, Richt has had a bright spotlight shining on him and his team, especially since they compete in the highly competitive SEC. In a conference known for its football, Richt has had to face tough critics from both the media and the stands regarding his decisions. When it comes to Georgia football, if things aren't going right, everyone's got an opinion and they aren't afraid to express it.

"It's part of the job," Richt said. "When you're in a leadership role, you're going to be criticized; that's all there is to it. But you can't shy away from leadership because of what people might say."

When it comes to criticism, Richt has learned to keep his cool. A Christian since his days as a grad assistant at Florida State

University, Richt has allowed the Lord to use this public scrutiny to shape him as a man of faith and to make him a better leader.

In Scripture, there is another Man who experienced a great deal of criticism: Jesus Christ. During His time on earth, Jesus raised more controversy than anyone ever had or ever would, and He certainly heard about it. Pharisees and leaders of the day continually confronted Him with their opinions, and more than once, Jesus even had to escape physical harm when He said something they didn't like.

> **"When you're in a leadership role, you're going to be criticized; that's all there is to it. But you can't shy away from leadership because of what people might say."**

But criticism came with the territory, and Jesus didn't let it sidetrack Him from speaking the truth and pursuing the mission His Father had given Him. Instead, He spoke confidently in front of His audiences, making bold statements that included revealing Himself as the Messiah—the unprecedented declaration that ultimately resulted in His crucifixion. But not even inevitable death could keep Him from speaking what He knew was right and true.

In life and sports, we all face critics. Everyone has an opinion about our performance, and many times they will share it with anyone who will listen. Part of the reason talk radio is so popular is because of its ability to scrutinize athletes, coaches, or leaders in general in a way that is pleasing to the audience. Internet bloggers say whatever is on their mind and, with the click of a button, they can trash a person to an unlimited population. From local papers to national TV shows to local coffee shop counters, critical commentary is as natural as discussions about the weather.

Christians experience similar criticism simply by choosing to follow Christ. Not everyone agrees with us regarding the deity of Jesus, and they are often willing to voice their personal opinions on both our faith and our sanity. But if we truly believe that Jesus is the Son of God, we can't allow these disparaging voices to keep us from speaking what we know to be true or from living in a way that honors Him.

In Matthew 16:24, Jesus said to His disciples, "Whoever wants to be my disciple must deny themselves and take up their cross and follow me." While the vast majority of us will not have to endure a literal cross like Christ did, we read here that believing in Him comes with a price.

When we receive Jesus Christ as Lord and begin living for Him, we will have to learn to bear the burden of criticism. It's part of denying ourselves earthly comfort in order to do what we know is right: living as His disciples and staying focused on things of eternity instead of things of earth. But the good news is that we will be rewarded for staying true to Him in the face of scrutiny. In Matthew 5:10–11, Jesus said that those who were persecuted on His behalf would be blessed. It's just a matter of facing it courageously and handling it with love (Romans 12:14).

Today if you truly desire to be your best for God, face your critics with peace and kindness knowing that you are receiving rewards more valuable than any accomplishment. You may not see them now, but when your brief time on earth is over and you begin eternity with the Father, these spiritual rewards will prove to be the most priceless trophies of all.

> ## Your Turn

How do you handle criticism? _____

_____

_____

How does that compare to how Jesus handled it? _____

_____

_____

How does an appropriate response to criticism reveal Christ to

the world? _____

_____

_____

How can you better reflect Christ the next time you are criticized

in sports, life, or matters of faith? _____

_____

_____

> **Being Your Best for God:**
> **Face your critics with courage.**

stats that last

*Religion that God our Father accepts as pure
and faultless is this: to look after orphans and
widows in their distress and to keep oneself
from being polluted by the world.* —James 1:27

NAME: Matt Holliday

TEAM: St. Louis Cardinals

POSITION: Outfielder

HIGHLIGHTS: MLB All-Star (2006–2008, 2010)
NL Batting Champion (2007)

No question about it, Matt Holliday has great stats. Major League Baseball is full of guys who would love to post his numbers. But contrary to the stereotype, Holliday is a team-focused guy who understands that people matter more than home run totals and slugging percentages.

"The relationship part of athletics is much more important than the stats," Holliday said. "At the end of your career, I think you'd rather have somebody say something positive about your character than about how well you threw a ball. God calls us to interact with people, and relationships are the important part in this life."

It would be easy for a guy with Holliday's bio to walk around a clubhouse like he owned it. During his big-league career, he has consistently ranked in the top ten in major hitting categories, including a banner year in 2007 in which he topped the National League in batting average, hits, and RBIs. His on-field performance has earned him multiple All-Star selections as well as a handful of Silver Slugger Awards. With a résumé like that, it would be easy for him to lose focus, but Holliday has kept his eyes fixed in a very specific direction—one that helps him keep his cleats on the ground.

"I just try to put it in perspective," he said. "I try to honor God and play for Him and my teammates. If I can help the team, then that's a good thing, and that mindset keeps me from getting too high or too low."

Keeping sports in proper perspective is one of the hardest things for athletes to do. At one point or another, we all get consumed with pursuing good stats, sometimes to the point of being trapped in sports idolatry—making the sport a virtual god. While it's natural to want to do well, we often get so wrapped up in being the best on paper that we forget what it means to be the best in the eyes of the Lord.

Instead of focusing on Him, many of us—athletes as well as regular joes—tend to get performance-centered tunnel vision. We become anxious or get in such a hurry that we don't even consider the people God has placed around us. We focus only on getting an edge by improving our bodies, our minds, or our image. Rarely do we consider the fact that the Lord might have a higher purpose for us than just playing to win.

> "I try to honor God and play for Him and my teammates. If I can help the team, then that's a good thing, and that mindset keeps me from getting too high or too low."

Take a look at James 1:27. It says, "Religion that God our Father accepts as pure and faultless is this: to look after orphans and widows in their distress and to keep oneself from being polluted by the world."

According to Scripture, the stats that matter to God have more to do with how we treat others than how we rank on any kind of stat sheet. Our numbers aren't what He calls pure and faultless; our love for others is. There may not be widows and orphans in our lives, but there are hurting people around us who are waiting for someone to take the time to share the healing truth of Christ—if only we would slow down and take our eyes off ourselves and our personal goals long enough to notice. It's not an easy thing to do, but if we truly believe that our lives—and our goals—are in God's hands, we can obey His others-focused plan and trust that He will take care of our performance and the results.

Today, instead of adopting a stat-focused, performance-driven mentality, learn to be your best for God by opening your eyes to His plan for you. Embrace His higher purpose of loving and serving others with the love He has given you. Then, like Matt Holliday, let the numbers speak for themselves as you focus on notching stats of a more lasting kind—hearts healed and lives won for eternity.

Your Turn

Being totally honest, what are your top three priorities in life?

Where does God rank on that list? Where do you place others?

Write out a list of priorities you think God would want for you.

Is there a difference between your list and God's? If so, what needs

to change? _____

Being Your Best for God:
Don't get tunnel vision.

intentional
teaching

Therefore go and make disciples of all nations, baptizing them in the name of the Father and of the Son and of the Holy Spirit, and teaching them to obey everything I have commanded you. —Matthew 28:19-20

NAME: Sue Semrau

TEAM: Florida State University

POSITION: Head Women's Basketball Coach

HIGHLIGHTS: Winningest women's basketball coach in FSU history

Rarely had photos of beautiful women in dresses caused such a stir, but this was a unique situation. These weren't fashion models or celebrities; they were college basketball players.

In 2009 Florida State University launched a women's basketball website that featured photos of the team's players wearing dresses and heels instead of uniforms and athletic shoes. As soon as the media discovered the site, a virtual firestorm of unpredicted controversy erupted. Why did they need to wear dresses? Were they trying to make a statement? What was their motive?

At the center of it all sat Seminole Head Coach Sue Semrau, who soon found herself addressing tough questions about beauty, identity, and femininity in sports.

"People say that any press is good press, and this definitely drove a lot of people to our site," said Semrau, FSU's head coach since 1997. "God knew what would happen, so we used it as an opportunity to teach life lessons to our players."

While Semrau may not have expected the controversy, she did her best to handle it with wisdom. As the media's questions came in, she opened the lines of communication with her players on the sensitive subjects and embraced an opportunity to help them grow. And because many of these conversations involved sensitive subjects, Semrau often turned to her go-to source of wisdom: the Bible.

Said Semrau, "If we know the truth, then that's what we're going to continue speaking."

As a Christian coach, Semrau knows her limits when it comes to sharing her faith. But when situations arise that mandate she share her personal beliefs, she speaks from her heart—not forcefully, but honestly.

> **"If we know the truth, then that's what we're going to continue speaking."**

Just like they do for coaches like Semrau, teachable moments come to all of us on a daily basis. Situations constantly arise, often unexpectedly, that can open the door for us to reveal more about Christ and His love to others. These include everything from media controversies like the ones at Florida State to everyday occurrences like spur-of-the-moment arguments. In fact, if we get into the habit of it, almost any situation can become a teachable moment if we embrace it as a chance to model Christ.

When Jesus left earth, He left clear instructions for His followers. In Matthew 28:19–20, we find what is called the Great Commission: "Therefore go and make disciples of all nations, baptizing them in the name of the Father and of the Son and of the Holy Spirit, and teaching them to obey everything I have commanded you." With these words, Jesus not only instructed believers to make disciples but also to teach them how to live for Him.

No one automatically knows how to live for Christ; it's a daily learning process that involves uncovering His mysteries and spiritual truths. Therefore, those who are experienced in the ways of the Lord need to come alongside those new to the faith and help them learn what it involves.

After we receive Christ, we receive this calling to teach others as He teaches us. The challenge for many of us comes in being intentional to seize those instructional opportunities as they surface. In Semrau's case, she could have continued educating her athletes with on-the-court lessons and handled the media controversy on her own. But instead, she engaged her athletes in the situation and allowed them to learn from the experience.

Part of being our best for God involves embracing our role as teachers. While that may sound intimidating, we don't have to be theology scholars to make a difference. When it comes to instructing others, God desires little more than a willing spirit. If we follow His prompting and engage others on matters of faith through everyday situations, He promises to give us the wisdom we need through the power of the Holy Spirit and the reinforcement of His Word.

Today, open your eyes and look for moments to teach others about God's truth. Try starting a conversation with someone that could spark a spiritual discussion. Pray for direction as you do, and trust the Holy Spirit to guide your words. You don't have to be a gifted speaker, just take the opportunity when it arises, share from your heart, and speak the truth you believe.

Your Turn

Have you ever thought of yourself as a teacher? Why or why not?

_____

_____

Do you shy away from spiritual discussions? Why? _____

_____

_____

In Matthew 10:19–20, Jesus said to His disciples, "At that time you will be given what to say, for it will not be you speaking, but the Spirit of your Father speaking through you." What does that say to you about the power of the Holy Spirit in conversation?

_____

_____

_____

_____

Being Your Best for God:
Seize the teachable moments.

set apart

You are the light of the world. A city situated on a hill cannot be hidden. —Matthew 5:14 hcsb

NAME: Brian Roberts

TEAM: Baltimore Orioles

POSITION: Second Base

HIGHLIGHTS: Two-time MLB All-Star (2005, 2007)

The desire to stand out from the crowd is something we all have in common. Deep down, we all want to be noticed and sometimes even fear never rising above mediocrity.

That inner desire to be distinct is one reason many of us play sports. We want to be unique and do something different—or better—than others, and the higher we rise in a sport, the more we naturally set ourselves apart.

As a two-time major league All-Star, second baseman Brian Roberts knows what it's like to stand out. In his time with the Baltimore Orioles, he's become the virtual face of the ballclub due to the powerful combination of talent and tenure. Where Roberts is different from many athletes, however, is in his desire for distinction. While most athletes covet fame from the field, Roberts prefers that his notoriety be spiritual. He'd rather stand out for Christ than stand out for stats.

"I'm here for God," Roberts said. "My job is to glorify Him with every second of every day and to plant seeds wherever I am."

Throughout his career, Roberts has been up front about his faith in both words and actions. He's spoken at faith-based events, shared his testimony in the media and has served the community hands-on, all of which has given him a spiritual spotlight—the kind that not only opens Christians up to persecution but also goes against that human desire to be revered by others.

For Roberts, however, it's a choice and a lifestyle he's willing to pursue out of his love and reverence for the Lord.

"When we struggle with whether we should fit in with the world or honor God, we're basically saying who is more important to us," Roberts said. "Is it more important that people like me, or is it more important that God looks at me and says, 'Well done, my good and faithful servant'?"

> **"Is it more important that people like me, or is it more important that God looks at me and says, 'Well done, my good and faithful servant'?"**

If we want to be our best for God, we need to be prepared for the distinction that comes with it. By living a Christ-honoring, Scripture-based lifestyle, we automatically set ourselves apart from the world around us. While other Christians and a handful of non-believers might support our godly lifestyle, many others will not. Because our ways will contrast their own, they may mock us, gossip about us, or just flat-out not like us.

In those times of opposition, it's important that we stay focused on Christ. After all, He did warn us that we'd have trouble in the world (John 16:33) and that it would hate us because of Him (John 15:18). But, whether we realize it or not, this hostility can actually be a good thing. When we are persecuted for making God-honoring choices, it often indicates that we're living out our calling of rising above sin and darkness.

In Matthew 5:14, Christ likened believers who operated outside of a sinful lifestyle to sources of holy radiance, calling them the "light of the world." According to Him, Christians shine with His glory, and like hilltop cities, cannot be hidden.

No doubt about it, we will be distinct if we are living for Jesus Christ. And it will take guts to be a "city on a hill" and endure the persecution of peers. In order to survive these situations and not give in to what's going on around us, we must believe that God is faithful and know that He has our back.

"Taking a stand for the first time may be hard," Roberts said. "It may be miserable, and you may lose a friend or a group of friends. But through standing up, you realize you can trust Him. The more you go through it and continue to trust Him, the more He proves faithful, and the easier it becomes."

The desire to be set apart is inside us all. God made us that way. At your core, you know that you were made for more than mediocrity, and when that desire is properly surrendered to the Lord, it can translate into your becoming a source of His light in even the darkest places.

Your Turn

If you could choose to be famous for one thing, what would it be?

How does being a Christian automatically make you stand out?

_____

_____

_____

Have you been persecuted for your faith? In what ways? _____

_____

_____

_____

How does your lifestyle differ from those who don't share your faith? Should there be a greater difference? _____

_____

_____

_____

Being Your Best for God:
Stand up and stand out for Christ.

taking
the lead

If it is to encourage, then give encouragement; if it is giving, then give generously; if it is to lead, do it diligently; if it is to show mercy, do it cheerfully. —Romans 12:8

NAME: Tommy Tuberville

TEAM: Texas Tech University

POSITION: Head Football Coach

HIGHLIGHTS: 2004 AFCA Coach of the Year
(Auburn University)

When Coach Tommy Tuberville arrived at Auburn University in 1998, he knew he needed to assemble a talented coaching staff in order to develop a successful football program. He hired experienced men for the typical offensive and defensive coaching positions, but then Tuberville took it one step further.

Once he had his on-field coordinators, he went in search of a "spiritual coordinator"—a full-time chaplain who could address the deeper needs of his players, coaches, and support staff. Tuberville was so concerned with their well-being that he hired Chette Williams, a local pastor and staff member of the Fellowship of Christian Athletes (FCA), to help them stay healthy in ways that had nothing to do with wrapped ankles or ice bags.

"We wanted them to mature as eighteen- to twenty-one-year-olds and to learn from their time here, not just in academics or sports," said Tuberville, whose own Christian faith has marked his coaching tenure. "We wanted to give them a light and a way to know that there was more to life than just football or academics."

Because it was a public university, Tuberville knew he couldn't mandate spiritual participation, but he also knew he had certain privileges when it came to running a program the best way he knew how. For Tuberville, that involved making spiritual aid readily available should any player desire it. Based on his own experience, he understood the power of a relationship with Christ and wanted those in his program to have the opportunity to embrace it for themselves.

"There are a lot of things that are cultivated through a football team in college," Tuberville said. "We felt like cultivating them through FCA and Jesus Christ was an avenue that would allow them to grow in all areas."

When he hired a full-time chaplain, Tuberville made a bold and compassionate move. He knew he was in a position to impact the lives of young men, and he wasn't willing to let that opportunity pass him by. For Tuberville, true success involved more than numbers on a scoreboard; it encompassed graduation rates, healthy team dynamics, and the maturity of men who would leave his program with a chance to succeed beyond the gridiron. By also making a spiritual coordinator available, Tuberville gave his athletes the chance to discover the most life-changing relationship of all: a saving relationship with Jesus Christ.

"We wanted to give them a light and a way to know that there was more to life than just football or academics."

For those of us who want to be our best for God, we would do well to follow Tuberville's example of maximizing our positions of influence to make a difference in the lives of others. Once we acknowledge Christ as our Lord, we are given the responsibility of sharing His truth and love with those around us. Essentially, we become His representatives here on earth.

This lesson is exceptionally important for those in positions of leadership, including those in sports. Because we are in positions of influence, we are able to communicate Christ to an attentive audience through the way we live and lead. People look to leaders for examples and, whether they realize it or not, often adopt the leader's characteristics and beliefs based on sheer respect for the position. Thus, when we find ourselves in these roles, we have the opportunity to offer our faith to others—not in a forceful way, but by modeling Christ's love and bringing Him into our teams.

Today, whether you find yourself in a current position of leadership or are just aiming to take one in the future, ask God how He wants you to bring others to Him in the process. Maybe you'll be the one to start a Bible study or hire a spiritual coordinator. Maybe you'll pray with an hurting teammate, coworker, or friend. Who knows? The bottom line is that, as long as you say yes to God when He calls you to act, you can know you're standing tall in your leadership role and ruling with His blessing.

Your Turn

What is your current sphere of influence? _____

_____

_____

_____

_____

Do you hold any positions of leadership? If so, what are they?

_____

_____

_____

_____

How can you embrace them as opportunities to convey the love and truth of Christ? _____

_____

_____

_____

_____

In what ways—both subtle and obvious—is God asking you to stand for Him? _____

_____

_____

_____

_____

Being Your Best for God:
Lead **your team to Christ.**

the whole truth

For when I preach the gospel, I cannot boast, since I am compelled to preach. Woe to me if I do not preach the gospel! —1 Corinthians 9:16

NAME: Ben Zobrist

TEAM: Tampa Bay Rays

POSITION: Right Fielder

HIGHLIGHTS: 2009 MLB All-Star

Ever hear the phrase, "a half-truth is a whole lie"? What about the often-quoted courtroom question, "Do you swear to tell the truth—the whole truth and nothing but the truth—so help you, God?" More than just hearing them, you've probably used them yourself.

In both statements, there is one key word that drives home a major point. It is the word "whole." Through its use, we find that, unless we are telling the entire story in any given situation, we're not telling the real story at all.

Major league All-Star Ben Zobrist has made it his life's mission to tell the truth—a specific message he learned at an early age about Jesus Christ coming to earth to seek and save the lost. From Zobrist's God-given platform as a pro athlete, he is given many opportunities to speak in front of groups. And, in each case, he knows that he is called to share the full gospel of Christ—not sugar-coating it to lessen controversy, but bringing the weight of the salvation message in its entirety.

"Everyone wants us to give a message about hard work and character, but the message we carry is an exclusive message—one about Christ and His mystery," Zobrist said. "I want people to know that everything good in me comes from Him and not my own effort."

As Christians, we are all given opportunities to share what Christ has done in our lives. Part of the reason God transforms us is so that we can share our redemption stories with others who need to experience it for themselves. But because we fear offending our listeners, we are often tempted to water down the message of Christ in order to make our words more acceptable.

Unfortunately, when we give in to this fear, the whole point of the message is lost. In fact, the results actually become counterproductive spiritually. Instead of learning about Christ's salvation and love, people mistakenly get the idea that simple human effort is sufficient. They walk away believing they can work their own way out of any situation and make self-improvements that will fix all of their problems.

> **"I want people to know that everything good in me comes from Him and not my own effort."**

In reality, self-improvement won't save anyone from eternal separation from God. Accepting Jesus Christ, receiving His salvation, and choosing to live for Him is the only way to secure our eternity with Him in heaven. And when we know that truth but fail to share it when communicating our stories, we rob others of the opportunity to inherit eternity for themselves.

Ben Zobrist knows that the blessings he's received in life are directly from God. He also knows that with those blessings has come a responsibility to share a message of salvation through Jesus Christ. If he chooses not to state it clearly and entirely, the whole point of his athletic platform will be null and void.

"I know that I've glossed over it in the past," he said. "I've failed to mention sin and what Christ has done for me in taking my penalty on Himself. The last thing I want people to do is to come away from a message about Christ thinking that it's just about me trying to become a better person. Christ didn't come just to make us better people. He came to die for us and to let us know that *He* was the better person."

Just like Zobrist, if you truly desire to be your best for God, you need to understand the weight of the message you carry. It's one of incredible value and importance, but it will only make an impact when you are willing to share it in its entirety. You can't worry about whether or not it makes others uncomfortable when you speak the name of Christ; your role is simply to tell the truth—the whole truth and nothing less.

Your Turn

When are you most tempted to gloss over the truth about Jesus Christ and His power in your life? _____

_____

_____

_____

What is the worst thing that could happen if you were to share your story and include the truth about Christ? _____

_____

_____

_____

Imagine standing before the Lord at the end of your life and having to account for the times you took credit for achieving blessings and success through your own hard work. What do you think He would say? _____

_____

_____

_____

How would you feel in that moment? _____

_____

_____

_____

_____

Being Your Best for God:
Tell the whole truth of Christ.

About the Author

As the editor of the Fellowship of Christian Athletes' (FCA) *Sharing the Victory* (STV) magazine, Jill Ewert has spent nine years communicating stories of faith from the world of sports. Through STV, she has interviewed many of today's leading Christian athletes and coaches and has covered a number of tough issues facing today's competitors. As a journalist, Ewert also has spent time in front of the camera, pioneering STV's online video series in 2006, and serving as an occasional field reporter for FCA. (Videos available at sharingthevictory.com.) Ewert is an avid runner and currently lives and works in Kansas City, Missouri.

Sharing the Victory Magazine

As the national publication of the Fellowship of Christian Athletes, *Sharing the Victory* strives to inform and inspire coaches, athletes, parents, and fans with stories of faith on the field and in the locker room. After celebrating twenty-five years of ministry in 2007, STV continues to cover positive Christian role models from athletics of every level, while also addressing tough issues facing today's athletes and coaches.

Many of the quotes in this book were originally obtained through STV interviews and are used with permission from FCA. For more information, including in-depth stories on the featured athletes and coaches, visit sharingthevictory.com.

Fellowship of Christian Athletes

"The Heart and Soul in Sports"

The Fellowship of Christian Athletes is touching millions of lives for Christ...one heart at a time. Since 1954, FCA has been challenging coaches and athletes on the professional, college, high school, junior high, and youth levels to use the powerful medium of athletics to impact the world for Jesus Christ. FCA is the largest interdenominational, Christian sports ministry in America and focuses on serving local communities by equipping, empowering, and encouraging athletes and coaches to make a difference for Christ.

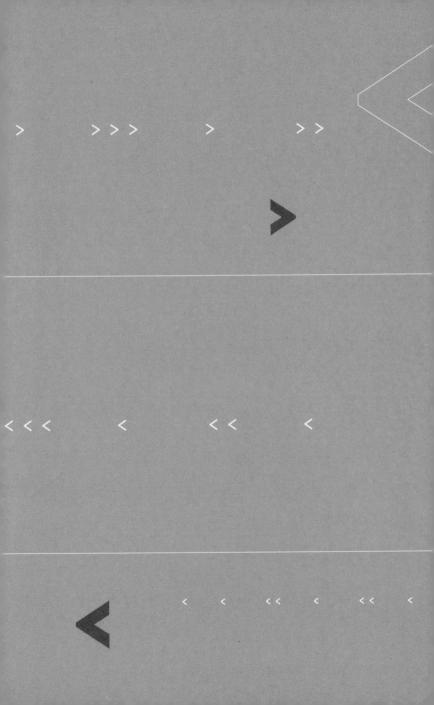

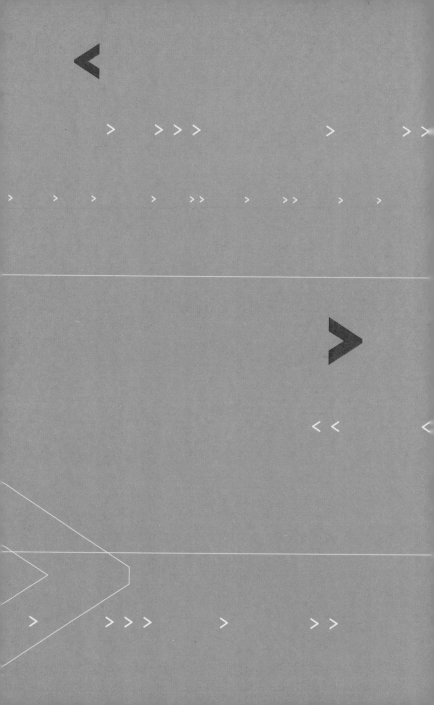